The Master Moves

by

MOSHE FELDENKRAIS

Meta Publications
P.O. Box 565
Cupertino, California 95014

Library of Congress Card Number 84-061647
I.S.B.N. 0-916990-15-X

MOSHE FELDENKRAIS
1904–1984

It was an honor to know you.
A joy to share your friendship,
  and a privilege to publish your books.

Richard Bandler

ACKNOWLEDGMENTS

Carl Ginsburg for his editing and for keeping the sound of Moshe in the manuscript.

Edna Sott for transcribing the original workshop tapes.

Anat Baniel and Mark Reese for their editorial assistance.

Bonnie Freer, photographer, for all the photographs of Moshe in this book.

Kolman Korentayer for his advice and editorial assistance on the photographs, text, and style of this book.

Richard Bandler
Publisher

THE META INTRODUCTION

I am looking at the picture of Moshe and I walking down the path to the swimming pool at the Mann Ranch and remembering the many paths we traveled together, the times we shared, and our beginnings.

I really loved and cared for him in a special way. He once said that time and love are interchangeable: those you love, you have time for. My availability for Moshe was timeless. You may ask, what qualities would earn this kind of caring and devotion?

When I first met Moshe it was at his office in Tel Aviv, a very modest place—one assistant, his first, Mia Segal; two worktables; a few stools to sit on; a small desk, and his special joy—paintings by his mother adorning the walls.

He invited me to sit in his office and watch him work with his clients. He called them "students" because they were learning a new way of functioning. During this visit of two months, I observed him working with over 100 people, many of whom had serious movement difficulties, such as strokes, cerebral palsy, etc. In every case their situation improved during the time that Moshe worked with them.

While in Tel Aviv I had the opportunity to have a series of lessons with Moshe myself. The impact of these lessons was profound: I moved differently; I felt better; my thinking became richer and clearer. I decided then and there to make myself available to Moshe for the purpose of assisting him in getting his work out into the world.

I went back to the U.S. and organized the first of an annual series of lectures, workshops, and teaching programs—and thus began the Moshe-Kolman Road Show.

It was a great adventure traveling with him, watching him

grow and change, and observing the effect he was having on people. During the workshops many participants would come up to tell him of the miraculous changes that happened to them during the Awareness Through Movement lessons.

Our travels took us from Coast to Coast, to such places as Esalen Institute in Big Sur to the U.S. Congress in Washington; to meetings and friendships with such people as Margaret Mead, Karl Pribram, Heiz M. Von Foerster, Jonas Salk, Milton Erickson, and Gregory Bateson, plus the many thousands who attended his workshops, and over 400 who are now practitioners of his work.

On our travels one of the places we looked forward to most was the Mann Ranch, presided over by Larry Thomas. After those large lectures with hundreds of people, the intimacy of the ranch enabled Moshe to share his work with ease and joy. There were usually 25 participants in the program, and since we all lived in the big house together, Moshe got to know everyone personally. Out of these five-day sessions with their special warmth and character, emerged a unique workshop which Moshe felt presented the essentials of his work.

The book you are about to experience *is* this workshop.

Welcome to the masterful and moving world of Moshe Feldenkrais.

This and more are my memories.
Thank you Moshe.

Kolman Korentayer

CONTENTS

INTRODUCTION

Carl Ginsburg

I attended my first Feldenkrais workshop during the summer of 1974. It was taught by a man who spent only a month with Moshe Feldenkrais and was not a qualified teacher of the Feldenkrais method. Nevertheless he had absorbed enough of the Feldenkrais spirit to convey something of the essence of Moshe's work.

I was at that time suffering from periodic bouts of low back pain and exploring various body therapies to alleviate my trouble. But I was initially reluctant to try Feldenkrais work. Feldenkrais movement, I had heard, had something to do with coordination. I knew I had poor coordination and I thought of myself as clumsy, without grace, a poor athlete and a terrible dancer.

The workshop was a revelation. In two days I discovered that I had all the ability to change what I wanted changed. It was possible for me to dance and move freely. I could stand in gravity and my pelvis could be underneath my shoulders. Above all I could do simple movements that would allow me to lengthen shortened muscles as long as I moved with what Feldenkrais called awareness.

As I no longer suffered with disabling muscle spasms in my back, I spent the next months talking of nothing but Feldenkrais work. During the winter, I heard that Feldenkrais himself was organizing a professional training group in San Francisco the following summer. I immediately applied; I was sure Moshe had answers for much of what I wished to understand.

Moshe arrived the first day of the training with essentially the same baggy trousers, the same open shirt we would see for the next three summers of training. His round pixie-like face combined with the two shocks of white hair on either side of his bald head gave him the air of a gentle but authoritative father. He walked slowly to protect his injured knees, the problem that led to his discoveries, but he was solid and balanced. As he sat facing the class in the center of the room we were suddenly under his spell.

Moshe always sat in the center facing his students. It produced a situation of authority whereby Moshe dominated what happened in the group. But it was an authority to create a context for learning. For his intent was always to provoke people to experience themselves directly and to make judgments and discernments out of that experience. When he challenged, it was on the basis that the person challenged had not used his or her own capacity to think and find out what is correct through experience and exploration. His authority was never authoritarian.

In our group Moshe was quite deliberate with what he did. For example, his mood shifts were very functional for getting us to learn. He had moments of great sweetness and would tell stories with a wise twinkle in his eye. Then he would be cajoling or mocking. Flashes of anger were at times as useful to waking us up as his moments of softness. He had a vast store of knowledge to draw on as well as a bundle of jokes. In fact he kept us alive to learning through the entire time we spent with him.

Above all he was the consistently keen observer of all that we did on the floor in front of him down to the tiniest nuance of expression in movement. From across the room in a group of sixty-five people, he would notice the person who moved in a way that revealed something interesting or different. In that way his group teaching was also individual teaching, for he would direct his comments often to one person without necessarily revealing that he was doing so. Then again he might choose to single out one person for attention with the intent that both the person and the group would benefit.

As I remember so many times how engrossed I became in Moshe's explanations and stories, I now suspect that I spent a great deal of time with him in trance. It was the kind of trance in which a lot of learning took place. Moshe was fond of saying that what you truly learned best would appear to you later as your own discovery. He knew clearly that the process of learning itself was not conscious, and that the success in learning something important and new lay in the nature of the experience inducing the learning—thus the stories, the shifts in tone and intonation, the mood shifts, the laughter and all the other accoutrements of his teaching style.

He was also a master at undermining our educated capacity to substitute verbiage for thought. He would ask, for example, why a particular movement would be easier with the body arranged one way as contrasted with another. But then he would show us that our answers did not match our experience. For Moshe thought and action were one. Or I should say that thinking necessarily results in a change in one's action.

In this transcript of Moshe's five-day public workshop at Mann Ranch in northern California in 1979, the full range of his thinking and his teaching style can be explored. All his major ideas on movement, human development, sensitivity, awareness, and so forth are presented both as exposition and exploration through movement lessons. These lessons, part of his unique contribution to human development, are the key to understanding the Feldenkrais method. There are both old and new lessons presented here. But the lessons that may be familiar from previous Feldenkrais books are taught in a new way. In a workshop situation Moshe inevitably explored his teaching process, both to pace and move with the group, but also to evolve the ideas he was presenting.

The lessons then are a "string of beads." The logic of presentation was not thought out ahead of time, but neither was it arbitrary. There was a very clear evolution of learning which was also specific for a particular group. Nor was the strategy of presenting the lessons verbally an accident. If one listens to a tape of Moshe directing a group, everything is clear. In inspecting a written transcript, however, it becomes immediately obvious that Moshe was a master of the half sentence and the incompleted thought. By leaving something unsaid,

Moshe pushed the listener to participate and complete the thought.

While ideal for learning through hearing, such tactics are confusing on a written page. In editing the manuscript for presentation in book form, I chose to complete sentences based on information presented a few moments later in the workshop. At the same time I have attempted to preserve the essence of Moshe's teaching style.

One further point about the lessons needs to be clarified. A person normally organizes himself or herself for action below the level of ordinary consciousness. But to focus one's attention on organization usually results in interfering with the process of changing organization. The same is true if one focuses attention on the goal of an action or movement. You will notice in reading the manuscript that Moshe never states the goal of what he is doing. So the lessons are designed to take attention away from a problem, but on the other hand to increase what Moshe calls awareness. Awareness in this sense is a kinesthetic knowing, a way of *feeling* the pattern that is needed.

The lessons therefore have no *content* about what is correct, but contain processes that allow you, perhaps for the first time, to feel and experience what is correct for yourself. The clue that you need for your own guidance, is to find a way to do what is asked that is easy, comfortable, and pleasant. In effect, you, yourself, will know through your increasing sensory ability how you have improved.

Moshe then was quite correct when he insisted that he was not a teacher and did not teach; that is, if teaching is taken to mean setting up a superimposed structure from outside oneself. Moshe as a teacher said repeatedly, "I want you to learn, but not to be taught."

Functional Integration, Moshe's hands-on work, exemplifies further the same way of changing. In this work, practitioner and pupil are in touch communication. The practitioner does nothing. But it is not the "nothing" of passivity. The practitioner feels what is necessary for the pupil's learning and through the double feedback loop, pupil and practitioner, the pupil experiences a new pattern of possibility. Such a communication requires a synchrony, and active linking of sensory and motor processes between practitioner and pupil, what Moshe called, "dancing together."

Again one could say that there is no teacher, only a learner and a context for learning and change provided by the practitioner. A Functional Integration lesson begins with the practitioner creating maximum comfort and support for the pupil and communicating through touch, a sense of safety. But the pupil may also be habitually holding, tensing, locking one part of the body with another. Feldenkrais' understanding of habit led him not to oppose this activity, but to support it by taking over the activity directly. Thus supported, Feldenkrais found, most pupils felt compelled to let go of the habitual action. A pupil was now ready for change and as Feldenkrais discovered, the mere suggestion of a new movement image was often enough to bring about a profound effect in the pupil's capability.

In this way, the problem of resistance is avoided altogether. But the gentleness of this approach depends upon a very cybernetic notion of how human beings control themselves. Feldenkrais' discoveries in this area were early on corroborated by his readings in the field of cybernetics, connected with his work in engineering and physics. And indeed his general approach was paralleled by similar discoveries by other pioneers in the general area of somatic teaching and therapy. His understanding of the importance of awareness, sensitivity and increased feedback parallels discoveries by Elsa Gindler as does his understanding of learning through increased inhibition of useless effort parallel the discoveries of F. M. Alexander. But perhaps the closest parallel in general approach to human communication and change is to the verbal therapeutic approach of Milton Erickson. Erickson too was focused primarily on his clients' changing patterns.

But as you read and interact with this book you may note some very unique aspects of the Feldenkrais work. For one thing, Moshe's emphasis is on the kinesthetic, feeling aspect of your self-organization. You may become aware as you explore the lessons, that Moshe guides you away from visualizing or verbalizing what you do until you have begun to have some kinesthetic experience of yourself in movement and action. Moshe's push towards the kinesthetic is based on his observation in himself and others, that the feeling and proprioceptive senses are the least trusted and the least attended to in our culture. His further observation is that profound change in the kinesthetic, feeling image of yourself results in change in all aspects of your self-organization.

A second unique aspect of Moshe's work is his insistence on function. Function in this sense is anything you do such as walking, standing, twisting, and so forth. A function is integrated when you carry it out with the whole of yourself, without self-interference. As you explore the lessons, you may become much more aware of the movement of your own structure in space, and the relation of parts of yourself, your pelvis and head for example, to the whole of your action. In the transcript Moshe emphasised some of these relationships. They are clues to a functional integration for yourself. But only your own experience can make his words clear to yourself. There is no learning in the Feldenkrais way without doing; i.e., doing the lessons.

Finally I wish to emphasize to you, the reader, that these wonderful movement lessons are the result of years of self-exploration on Moshe's part. There is a goldmine of material here, just in the few lessons presented in this workshop, for both the newcomer and the experienced practitioner. Each lesson, that seems so complete and perfectly constructed for learning, took hours of trial and error to develop. Now it is possible to generalize about how to create such a movement lesson. Moshe began only with his experience in Judo, his desire to improve his injured knees, and his inquisitive mind. Without guidelines, without a predecessor, but with an openness to his own experience, he made discovery after discovery. Now you, yourself have a chance to benefit. I wish you a hearty success.

HOW TO USE THIS BOOK

For the newcomer to Feldenkrais work I would like to give you some hints as to how to use the movement lessons to allow yourself as much change as is possible.

Moshe had a favorite old Chinese saying which he liked to quote:

> I hear and forget.
> I see and remember.
> I do and understand.

I can only encourage all readers to get on the floor and do the lessons. Some basic ways of going about this are in order:

First, each movement should be as easy, gentle and comfortable as slicing soft butter. The limit of your movement is the point at which you just begin to feel a slight tension or strain. If you move short of your limit, your learning will improve tremendously. As you will discover you can learn by doing almost nothing. But you must think through the action required kinesthetically, that is, through your feeling sense. There is one lesson in the book that proceeds almost entirely through thought in this way.

Second, you must go slow enough for your more slow-acting motor cortex, the part of your brain that organizes action, to catch up with what you are doing. When you go fast you evoke your automatic previously organized way of doing things. Here you want change and can get it through slowing down your movement one hundred or two hundred percent.

Third, what you do has to be enjoyable if you are to learn and change. When you get tired or restless, it's time to stop.

If you are enjoying yourself, you can keep going as long as you wish.

In the process of doing and paying attention in the way Moshe directs, you may experience sensations and then understandings that have eluded you before. Savor these experiences and remind yourself of them later. That way the changes you experience will more easily become part of your daily life.

The lessons in the manuscript may not be easy to do with a book in your hand. One possible solution is to read Moshe's directions on to a tape and play it back for yourself. Be sure in recording directions to give yourself enough time to complete each step. Each lesson is about forty minutes to an hour long.

One lesson is interrupted frequently with commentary. The commentary is so integral with the lesson you may want to record all of it to get the flavor of how Moshe integrates thought and action.

As you will gather from Moshe's words there is no extrinsic right or wrong way to do the lesson. The lesson is your opportunity to explore and find out what is right for yourself. And your guide is your own comfort, ease, and enjoyment. When things get difficult that is the time to stop and rest.

However, Moshe's instructions are quite specific. When he asks you to do some movement on the right side he means the right side. Working on the left side may well spoil the effect of the lesson. The execution of the lesson is done in your handwriting and with your own ease and comfort in mind. But "lift your right hip" or "bring your left elbow over your head" mean precisely what they say. If something feels uncomfortable to do, stop, find a way you can do what is asked that feels easy and possible. In some instances you may work in thought only. As Moshe stresses often in this workshop, you can always tear your muscles to get where you think you ought to be. You can once. But you will pay in pain and discomfort later. On the other hand, if you treat yourself with the respect you deserve, the benefit to you in greater ease and ability may be beyond your imagination and expectations.

One small help in following directions is to realize that Moshe's reference ground for movement is yourself and not your surroundings. Therefore, up means towards your head and down, towards your feet. If he intends you to lift towards the ceiling, he will say so specifically.

Use this book well and you will be surprised at the results. After trying the lessons, you can begin to explore on your own. You may then wish to explore the book again. On each re-exploration you may be surprised to find more and more available to your understanding. One of the great beauties of Moshe's work is the depth of material and understanding hidden in his seemingly simple words. There is more here than we can imagine.

Introductory Lecture: Detecting Small Differences

INTRODUCTORY LECTURE:
DETECTING SMALL
DIFFERENCES

It is usually very difficult to break the ice. Especially after you have eaten, I believe that work in that state is harmful. You may not feel it, but I can assure you that I have lived long enough to know that you pay for those things through the nose afterwards (laughter). Have you seen anybody sing well after eating? No, well, I normally don't eat before teaching, because I found that when I eat and then talk, and then I listen to myself later I think I shouldn't have done it. When you eat and work, it becomes difficult to tell rather small differences. And if you can't tell small differences, that complicates the work very much. You will find that in order to tell small differences you must have free choice. But first let's ask: what is a small difference and how can you tell?

Can anyone who is not a musician and cannot distinguish small differences, say whether Menuhin, Oistrach or Heifetz plays Beethoven's violin concerto best? Well, I am no musician. I never studied music in my youth, but I have a friend who is a great musician, the world famous conductor, Igor Markevich. I taught at his international course for orchestra conducting in Salzburg and Monte Carlo, a month each year for fourteen years. At his home we listened to recordings of these great violinists, and he tried to make me aware of which one was the best. Now if someone like Szegetti listened, he would distinguish enormous differences between the three. But how can you or I distinguish what for us are small differences? It's not so important to decide who is the better violinist. After I sat an entire evening with Markevich listening to three recordings several times over, I discovered that the best technician is Heifetz; he has the greatest facility and his work is faultless. But the greatest musician is Oistrach.

Let us look for a moment at what brought humanity to the state where we are able to distinguish small but significant differences. It is not a very impressive state, but it is better than the primitive state of humanity ten thousand years ago when people could not read or write. It's not that reading or writing are so important. But primitive language was poor and this meant that people's brains were undeveloped. Primitive people could only distinguish very big differences. They could say 'a fish', and 'thunder'. But for fine distinctions they had no way to express differences. What brought humanity to it's present state is, of course, the genetic inheritance of the human species. We have a brain which is very different from all other brains in the animal world. We won't go into the details now, but the human brain grows five times it's size at birth. A human brain at birth weighs about 350 grams, about the same as a chimpanzee or gorilla. But at the end of life an ape's brain is only 450 grams. But the human brain grows at an extraordinary speed from 350 grams to an adult brain which has something in the order of 1500 grams.

We are born with very few reflexes and instincts. The instincts of the human species are nearly non-existent. No human being can take a grass in his mouth and be able to tell by the taste whether it is poisonous. We don't know whether water is deadly for us or not. We can breathe air that is killing us and we don't feel it. Now, what things can a human being distinguish as well as any of the animals in the world who know enough to eat grass when they are constipated? What sort of instinct have human beings? Human beings can have children and hate them. Many humans have to learn to love their child. It's incredible. If you look at all the instincts you find that they are very tenuous, insignificant. But, the humans do have something, which is that they learn in a different way.

Animal species know what they have to do and how they are going to live. A beaver knows how to build a house without learning how. That is not quite true. Animals have to learn too, but very, very little compared with the human species. All mothers teach their progeny: ducks teach ducklings to swim, chickens teach chicks to pick grains and worms. Learning is essential. But the degree of learning that the human species uses for its own development is much larger. Compared with animals we have no instincts at all—only a capacity to learn.

If you look at any one of us here: what are the things that make us sociable so we can communicate with each other? If we love each other, hate each other, fight each other, or be in peace, we do that out of what we have learned. There is nothing which distinguishes one man from another that is more important than the learning he has done. For instance, we would not consider that a person is more important than another because he is five inches taller, or because he is blonde or because he is dark. But what he knows how to do, the way he speaks, makes a difference. A man doesn't speak like a dog who barks. And a Chinese dog can understand a San Franciscan dog quite well, and pee on the same telegraph pole in the same way and get the same information out of it. But if I pee on the post and a Chinaman comes and smells it, he wouldn't know a thing. Except that it stinks (laughter). We talk to each other, but not to a Chinaman. Why? Because a Chinaman has learned something else. As far as our social life goes, learning is the most important thing. You learn to write; no animal can write. But no one was born knowing how to write. There are about three thousand languages in this world and they're written in different alphabets and in different ways. And for each group the special language is learned. This doesn't happen with any animal in the world, not with ants, birds, fish, ducks, mosquitoes, viruses, bacteria.

And the same is true for walking. We humans walk in similar but different ways because we learn to walk. Animals walk instinctively. Ten black cats walk so alike that you won't be able to tell which cat you know. But, if you take ten different people, your father and brother among them, regardless of how they dress, and you see them walk in the street two hundred yards away, you will recognize your father or your brother though he's dressed *exactly* like someone else. How is that? It is because none of our gaits are similar. You can tell a person by his gait as precisely as by his fingerprint. No two people walk alike; yet all lions walk alike, all cobras crawl alike. They are so alike, that unless you are very familiar with them and study them and observe them you cannot tell a difference. But in a human being the difference is the most important thing. Why are there so many differences? How is it, of three billion people you can tell each one by his gait if you see him once.

Now, walking, writing, speaking are alike in that each person has a unique way of doing that activity. If you take ten dogs that you don't know and listen to their bark and try to discern their species, you'll find it extremely difficult to tell which dog barked because their barking is instinctive and reflexive. Therefore, dog barks are similar. Our barking is very different. Singing and thinking are also individual. No two people think alike, because they have learned their thinking through speaking. And very few actually think for themselves. That's another thing that must be learned. Many people learn mathematics, but to become a mathematician is to be able to think mathematics for oneself. There is not one in a thousand who learns mathematics who is a real mathematician in that sense. Therefore, you can see that most of the things that are important for the human species are learned.

Now, if it's so important, what is learning? Most people are concerned only with scholastic, academic learning, which is a kind of learning of relatively little importance. Scholastic learning is a matter of choice, a choice that you can take or not take. You could, for example, learn chemistry, but you could certainly make another choice. That is of little consequence to humanity as a whole. What is important to each of us is certainly not scholastic learning. Many of us here have never been to university. Many have learned at the university and they are not much better than the people who didn't. Sometimes worse. So, what is learning? What's the learning that is important?

There is, of course, an important kind of learning that we all know. What small children learn before the age of two is important to them for the rest of their lives. Of course, such learning depends also not only on the child, and heredity, the way of the double spirals of the DNA he has inherited, but on being a human being in a human society. The inherited part of us, what makes us a human animal, must be cultured, qualified by learning for us to become human beings. And that learning does include our personal learning from all the generations before. What you can teach a clever gorilla in a lifetime a human idiot learns in the first three weeks of his life. So you see, our learning is of the greatest consequence, because everything that is important to us as human beings living in a human society came by learning. Nobody can sing Shubert, or any other thing without prolonged learning. But any bird who sings a song doesn't have to learn. And you can't teach him another song.

Now, what's the learning that is so important for us? I have gathered about forty different definitions of learning through the years, and every one of them dealt with the kind of learning that you find among grown-up people, what I have called, scholastic learning. Of course, you can learn a telephone book by heart, or to solve cross-words, or to play chess. You can learn to become a doctor, a politician, an economist, a financial wizard. You can learn accountancy. You can learn so many things. None of them are universally important to all of us. Indirectly, of course they are, as far as the social organization goes. But on an individual basis, they are not important. What sort of learning *is* important? You find an incredible thing. Once you look at it very closely you find that the learning that enables you to do the thing you *know* in another way, and one more way, and then three more ways, is the learning that is important. And when you see learning in that light, you find that a whole world of important things is open to us.

Now what do I mean by learning to do a thing in two ways? If you learn to speak, you learn to do it in one way—"the correct way." The correct way is to say, "I love you." But you can say, 'I love you' (very softly), 'I love you' (strongly), 'I love you' (shrilly). You will find there are as many ways of saying 'I love you,' and each way is different. Each has an influence on the person to whom you speak. Thus for anything you do, speak, write, sing, if you can't do it in two different ways, you do not have free choice. And therefore, the truly important learning is to be able to do the thing you already *know* in another way. The more ways you have to do the things you know, the freer is your choice. And the freer your choice, the more you're a human being. Otherwise, you are like a computer who is switched on and can do very clever things, but only one way. So too with all the major lower animals, bacteria, viruses, and so forth. They act in the way they have inherited, and that's that—finished.

What do we mean by free choice? Let us go back to the question of who is best, Oistrach or Menuhin or Heifetz? The choice is difficult for the great majority of people, because they are unable to tell small differences. If Oistrach and I each play the fiddle, someone could say, "Yes, he plays better than you. Because you don't play at all. You're no good." When the difference is enormous there's no difficulty choosing. *But,* when you want to have human choice that's important to us as human beings, then you must have sensitivity, and be able to discern small differences. To do this you must improve and increase your sensitivity. That being so, how do we increase sensitivity?

Here is the secret. You cannot increase your sensitivity unless you reduce the effort. First a few idiotic examples: if you look at the sun, you cannot tell whether there is another bulb burning or not. Or can you look at the sun and tell me whether I shine a torch behind you? The sensitivity becomes *very small* when the stimulus is enormous. When the stimulus is enormous, you want to see the sun bursting, exploding— then you will see an increased light. Of if you go in the street during the day with some of the street lights burning, you don't notice that they are lit. So, if the stimulus is great, nothing doing, you can tell only very big differences. Therefore, your choice is not free—it's not a human choice.

Look, take other examples: Stand near an airplane with the engines running. If somebody bangs a gong, you can't hear it unless you're near the gong. In order to speak to someone, you have to come near and shout in his ear. If I carry a piano on my back and the birds drop something on the piano, I wouldn't know; I wouldn't feel a difference. And if somebody takes it away I wouldn't feel a difference either. Because compared with the effort the increase in weight is insignificant. What could drop so that I could feel the difference? Maybe an elephant (laughter).

Now, I can tell you a funny story. It's not about an elephant's dropping, although you know Fritz Perls had a clear distinction between chicken shit, bullshit and elephant shit: you see that's such an enormous difference that's not a human choice (laughter). In the beginning, after I wrote my book, *Body and Mature Behavior,* somebody in London thought that I must have known Heinrich Jacoby because he learned from Jacoby some of the things that he found in my book. Yet I never knew that Jacoby ever existed. He said, "It's impossible. You should meet." He wrote to Jacoby and sent him my book. A year and a half later I took my vacations and went to see Jacoby. I thought we would be interested in meeting each other. Does anyone here know who Heinrich Jacoby is? He is a very important teacher. He's dead now. But we were very great friends after that meeting; we met several times. But what I wanted to tell you is what he taught me that I taught him: something very funny. It has to do with sensitivity and what we are doing now.

I had a deaf ear all my life. I couldn't sing a thing. Even the national anthem I would sing only if a big crowd was about and they shouted at the top of their voice. I shouted at half of my voice and managed somehow to get through the national anthem. In the house where I was raised and in that part of

Russia we did not have music. The Russians themselves are musical and learn, but a Jewish family—anyway, it's a long story (laughter). The first time I whistled a tune, I was ticked off for doing like a goy (laughter). A Jew should do something which will raise your learning, your intelligence, but not whistle like a goy. Of course, when a boy of four or five whistles a tune he has learned, when he is ticked off like that by his father once or twice, then afterwards he has a deaf ear for the rest of his life. Now I wanted to undeafen my ear, but it turned out Jacoby was the one who gave me what I needed. He had a funny way of doing it. At the start he said, "Look, there is a Bechstein piano. Would you please play something?"

I said, "I can't play the piano."

He said, "That's why I asked you to play."

I thought that funny and said, "If I don't know how to play the piano how can I play the piano?"

"Well, play! Do you know a tune? Any tune." Now how could a man who doesn't dare to sing the anthem play a tune?

He said, "Well, just remember, anything in your life—don't you remember anything?" Then suddenly I remembered, something funny (sings a few bars) something that Rovina sang in the Song of Songs: 'You Are Beautiful My Beloved Wife;' something like that. I managed to produce it like an old croak without loosing the tune. But much better than I did now.

Anyway, he said, "Play it. It's a beautiful tune."

I said, "How can I play it?"

"Try." So I sat at the piano and began to bang the keys. Whatever I touched—do, re, mi, fa, sol, la, si—nothing fitted, nothing came out (laughter)! Bang, bang here, bang there. He listened patiently. By the way, I must tell you that Jacoby himself was the first musician that worked with Delcrosse, the man who developed Eurythmics. Has anybody done Eurythmics? Afterwards he was the director of the opera in Strasburg. He listened and listened and then after I had been at it for a few minutes he saw that nothing would come out of it and I felt completely idiotic.

He said to me, "This is a Bechstein. It's a good piano. What has it done to you? Why do you ruin it like that? What are you banging it for?" Well, I felt a bit ashamed and found actually that I was banging and hitting the keys and making a terrific noise.

Then he said, "You wrote in your book, *Body and Mature Behavior,* that by the Weber-Fechner Law, the stimuli and the responses to stimuli follow a logarithmic law. Therefore, in order to tell the difference with very loud noises you have to make a very big difference." And I, somehow couldn't understand. *I,* myself, wrote that if you want to have sensitivity you have to decrease the effort or the initial stimulus otherwise, you can't tell small difference. If the stimulus is great there must be a tremendous difference between that and the other just to detect it. In fact, I made people lie on the floor, so that they have nothing to do, and are not using muscles, and can, thereby, detect minor differences. In such a situation you may find that what you have done before can be done in a better way.

It turned out, strangely enough, when I began to touch the key and make the smallest noise that I could barely hear, and sang to myself (sings), I took about three minutes to find the tune and play it. And I had never played before. I had no prior idea how to go about it. I got another surprise. There are some teachers that are worth their weight in diamonds. They know things, and you don't know how they know it. While I was searching for the tune and playing it, he recorded my performance on a tape recorder, my first banging, and then the way of reducing the noise and searching, and finding the tune. Once I found the tune, having a good visual memory, I played it quickly and fast. But the whole bloody thing was recorded. So I learned something again that I remember until today, thirty-five years later. Jacoby made me listen to the tape recording. When I listened, I could hear banging and banging and nothing coming out of it, and then gradually something coming out, and I was astonished myself. The period when I searched for the tune, I made extraordinary good music. Then he had me notice that once I had learned the tune, I could play it, and increase the speed. When I heard the tape, I found with my deaf ear that I had played in such a way that no professional musician would be ashamed of playing like that.

Jacoby said, "That's real music. No musician can play better. I couldn't play it now better than you did because it was your discovery, and it was wonderful music. And now listen what you have done with it afterwards—look at the end when you repeated it."

Now the thing that is important in learning is not *what* you do but *how* you do it. Now that sounds crazy. If you play music it's not important which music you play, whether you play Bach or Gershwin or Shostakovich or Bartok, but *how* you play it. If you write a novel, it's not important what you write about. It could be about a love triangle. There are about ten million novels written like that. But it is the *how* that makes a Proust, a Tolstoy, or distinguishes the cheap novels that you just buy and throw away. It's *how* you write that's important. It's not what picture you paint. You may paint a night pot in a hospital, or a chair, like Van Gogh, or the ass of a woman. There are a million asses so painted (laughter). But very few are like Titian. There are thousands of pictures of women's breasts, but some of them are memorable pictures for the world. It depends how you paint and not what you paint. You can paint a squirrel like Durer. What's there to draw a squirrel? Now you have a look at that squirrel; it's the most squirrely squirrel that you know (laughter).

Now, let's go a bit back. Since you didn't record what I said, can you tell me, what did we talk about? Can you recall for a minute the steps. What is learning? What do you need in order to have free choice? Can you remember, or not? Think of it a minute. And you know, it's not a challenge. I will tell you what I said. If I challenge you nothing will come into your head; that's how it's done at school, where there is one idiot who says, 'I know' and the others don't, because they are challenged. But how do you develop, have the guts, and the security, and the ability to think? Now, try to remember what we said. But then don't try; just see whether you can remember any of the things that struck you—something you didn't like. Can you? And it doesn't matter if you can't. Don't think long. But now think of something you liked. Can you remember any of the stories I told. And if you can't I will repeat the whole thing again for you (laughter). I will repeat it so that you will know it.

And you will find that even the things you wrote down are futile, because while you wrote you were not listening and you don't know it now unless you read it again. When you do read it again, you will see that as you wrote while I was talking, it's written in a way that has meaning only while I'm talking. Later you won't know what you wrote there. Then you'll find learning means having at least another way of doing the same thing. Now I say that you won't understand what I have said unless you do it in your *experience*. I mean try something that you know and learn to do it in another way. We will do that in this workshop, and you will see that you will be astonished so deeply that you'll keep quiet. You won't say anything. Because it will be a real discovery, just like how I discovered to play the tune, though never in my life did I play the piano and didn't know how to do it. We will be learning to do the things you know in different ways in order to have a free choice. Without free choice, we have no human dignity.

People who don't have free choice don't respect themselves and feel inferior to everybody else and to themselves! Now, in order to have free choice we must have significant difference. And in order to have a significant difference you cannot increase the stimulus, but you can increase your sensitivity. And since sensitivity increases only when you reduce the stimulus, that means you reduce the effort. Therefore, anything that you learn with difficulty, with pain, with strain is futile; you will never use it in your life. That's why people go to school and don't remember a thing they have learned. Because they learned it under strain, under violence, in ways where they made tremendous efforts, and were ashamed, and were striving, and competed with one another, and even rehearsed it. That is not learning. It is exercise. Under those conditions you can do only one thing: repeat what you do as many times as you need to to satisfy the teacher. You end up giving the response that the teacher wanted—otherwise you don't pass. Repetitions, exercises, are a cuckoo business; you'll never learn anything out of it. The best you will do is to get familiar with one way of responding. You lose in that way any ability to improve.

You can see it now in America with jogging. People jog and jog and jog and I will bet you of all the joggers in America there won't be more Americans to win gold medals in running. Joggers exercise; they don't learn. They don't learn to run. If there were learning in exercise, then if you wanted to know arithmetic you should be sitting now and saying: four times five is twenty, fifty times. Why don't you do it? Why don't you have to exercise that? Because that was so learned that you know that you can get 20 in about 100 different ways.

If you listen to young children when they learn you can see that these things are so significant to them. You ask a boy who learns addition for the first time, "How much are four and six?"

He says, "nine."

You say, "what do you mean nine? You don't know how much 4 and 6?"

He says, "It can't be 10 because 10 is for 5 and 5." We don't see that—that 10 is already occupied by 5 and 5 (laughter). And therefore, we know 10 in at least a million different ways. We can get 10 through addition, subtraction, division, and multiplication of hundreds of different figures. And we have learned it like that and therefore it is indelible. Until you become dotty you will know it. That's the way of learning, not repetition. There's no difficulty. Nobody has to write it down or record it.

To increase your sensitivity, you must reduce the effort.

How do we reduce the effort? We are so used to making efforts, because in the struggle to become qualified, to be considered like everybody else, we must not only compete with each other but with ourselves. We make tremendous efforts at school. Those who don't make tremendous efforts are considered no good at all. They are no good in their own eyes for many years afterwards, even if they are clever. I believe all of us are more clever than we look (laughter). It's not a joke. We will see that most of you are able to learn much faster than you think you can. And you're not such idiots as you made of yourselves in school.

How do we reduce the effort? By doing what? Our parents and teachers say, "you could be someone if you would only make the effort, if you only wanted. Look, other children make an effort. They sit, and do, and become good pupils—and you are a silly ass. I pay for you, I work and teach you, and what happens? You make no effort." Therefore, unless we make efforts we don't deserve to learn anything, or be able to do anything. We get so used to that that we make efforts when it's not necessary. We make efforts that don't improve our learning; they improve our ability to suffer and expend energy futilely. Look at the pain that it does, the inconvenience, the harm that it does. What do we do then?

Effort—I'm speaking so loosely, but we will see that every one of those things cannot be explained in words, though you understand a little of what I mean. It's only when you have learned it on your own body, that you will see that to make a wider choice for yourself, you will have to increase your sensitivity, and reduce the effort. And you cannot reduce the effort without improving your organization. Now what does it mean, "improve your organization?" What sort of organization?

Ah. I have just reminded myself. What I did now was the worst thing a teacher can do. I stretched your attention to the point where one of you yawned. And since that person is not sillier than you or I, I assure you that in a minute many of you will yawn because your attention is tired out. So if I continue, you will increase your effort and strain and stop learning. Then you will say, "Oh, yes, I don't remember what he said. He was interesting. That's all (laughter)."

Now, to myself I was interesting if you can go and tell your beloved or your wife, "Listen, he said something about learning the thing I already know in a different way in order to have free choice. For that I must be able to tell *differences*. And the difference must be significant. But I can distinguish smaller differences, not by increasing the stimulus, but by reducing the effort. To do this I must improve my organization. And then he stopped." Can you repeat what I've said tonight? You see that everyone of you can, even those who haven't recorded or taken notes. Now I consider that an example of good learning, not of good teaching, but of good learning. Because the important thing is that you learn, not that I teach you. And if a teacher cannot make people *learn,* to my mind he is no teacher at all. I believe I am a good teacher (applause). And a good teacher must learn when to shut up (laughter). Thank you very much.

LESSON ONE:

TWISTING TO FLOOR

Stand with your feet about shoulder width apart. Relax your knees. Start to place your right hand, palm down, on the floor to the front and a little to the left of your left foot. Let your knees bend and twist to allow for an easy movement. Leave your feet in place. Touch the floor and return to standing many times until the movement is familiar. As you continue, follow the trajectory of your pelvis each time you go to the floor and return.

Now imagine, if you were to continue the same trajectory of your pelvis as you go past the position where your hand touches the floor, where would your knees go in space? What would your body do, and where would your pelvis finally land? The movement should be continuous, without stopping or reorganizing yourself at any point. After you have touched the floor, leave your hand on the spot you touched, and your feet at the same spots on the floor, but let your feet turn as you continue the trajectory and you will find yourself continuing to twist until you are seated cross-legged facing opposite to the direction in which you started. Now return to standing through the same pathway with your right hand in the same position on the floor as it was when you first touched to sit. The movement should repeat the same spiral motion upwards and your pelvis will move through the same trajectory. Note which leg ends up in front of the other each time you sit this way. When you have achieved a continuous movement up and down, try the movement on the other side placing your left hand on the floor this time. Think through what you need to do a few times before you start.

[At this point the tape continues as Moshe further explores the lesson.]

Decide in which direction you want to get up, and place your legs so that you can do it. Now you'll see that the direction of turning indicates which hand should help you and which leg, and how the legs should be placed. Marvelous? Can you see? You don't even have to roll. As soon as you think of your pelvis, it doesn't matter which leg, which arm is used. Your leg and pelvis form a continuous curve in the movement. And notice, your legs and arms will organize themselves as perfectly as can be; yet most teachers would insist when, and which hand and which leg. You know, you can do the movement as it should be, and that thought organizes each brain and each body. Now would you please stand up. This is more difficult. Decide which hand you put on the floor; that will determine to which side you will turn to sit. And you don't have to decide; when you place your hand, you'll find that the lower system remembers which way to turn and how to sit and what to do. In other words, you'll find that your ability to learn is a hundred fold better than what you could learn through exercise. As soon as you feel, sense, act and think at the same time, you find that in ten minutes you can learn as much as a hundred percent. Usually you'll find that as far as learning as I define it goes, the older, the more experienced and the wiser the person, the faster he learns. It has nothing to do with whether the person has arthritis, or heart disease, or any difficulty.

Now, take a minute to try for yourselves anything you want, to see what you could improve in your movement. While you do that, lift your head and look at the ceiling and stiffen your neck. Notice what happens to you and what happens to your breathing. You carry out the shape of the movement; yet it is idiotic. Obviously before, without knowing it, you used your head better than that; but in getting up you should be able to see the ceiling. Now how would you organize getting up and seeing the ceiling properly? Probably by your own sense of what is proper, after the experience. Do the same thing, but look at your sex while you get up. Again do the movement, and while doing it look from one person to another. That means from your sex to the ceiling, from the ceiling to your sex.

[One person, who has back pain, stops. He is sitting with his legs crossed and his knees far from the floor. Moshe comments.] You cannot do it. Then I say, if you will do it properly your back will improve, provided you don't do it as an exercise. Go as slowly as you can, finding out why and where you use your back in an idiotic way. You need not get up, bend from the idea of getting up. Your legs are not open. Do you know why they are not open? I would like you to see and find out where a functional integration will make a difference; where nobody in the world can do better than you're doing now. Now here is a person who was the first to get up, yet she has had pain in the back for the last six weeks. Now if you take an X-ray, you will find there's some narrowing of spaces between the discs, and that they will suggest either a corset, or if it gets worse, an operation. Now, look at her knees! Look at his knees! Can you see how far they are from the floor? Why is that so? Now watch. [Moshe asks the man he pointed out to round his back, and his knees draw closer together.] Look, his knees go up. Therefore, it is not the knees; it's the small of the back. Now let's see, what happened to the small of the back. Do not try to change it. The small of your back is painful because you are a lucky human being. The pain is showing you that if you did another few improper movements, you would make such a dreadful problem in your spine that you would not be able to straighten your legs and would suffer a paralysis. We are so constructed that we have pain first. The whole structure of the brain, spinal cord and spine in general is such that the sensory nerves are outside and the motor part is inside of the vertebrae. Between each of the vertebrae the motor and sensory roots join together and make the nerve. The pain causes you to inhibit your motor roots so that you cannot make the painful movement and damage the motor part of the nerve. If it were inverted, you would first have the paralysis, and then the pain. Pain shows you the way to improve, so that you can eliminate pain for the rest of your life.

Now, what is the thing that you have to learn? Sit with your legs crossed, one in front of the other and lean on your hands behind your pelvis. Try to lift your knees gently and do it ten times. Lift and let them go. Don't try to widen them. Now make a smaller movement, but faster like this—pap . . . pap . . . pap . . . make about thirty like that. Now observe your breathing.

Thirty movements more or less so that it becomes monotonous, and you interfere less and less with your intention. Slowly, move both feet a little bit away, and nearer to yourselves. Gently, only that part that feels nice. Are your knees more open than before? A little; that being so, see whether it's easier now to move the body a tiny little bit forward and back. Now change over now you cross your legs, and lift both knees again. Now stretch your knees gently, and slowly adjust your feet to bring them nearer to yourself. You can help with your hands. Put the right hand behind the other one on the floor as you move your feet. Now observe that while you do that movement, your pelvis rocks. Stop as you are and stand on both hands behind you, leaving your hand where it was. Now, in that position think without actually moving, that you are going to move your pelvis in such a way that the pressure on it will be on the forward part of the ischium. That means you push your stomach out a little bit and your head gets taller. Now do the opposite. And now do this movement a few times, gently. You will see that your trouble is actually not as low as the pain you experience, but higher in the dorsal part of your back. Continue forward and back many times. Let the movement regulate your breath. Now change your hands so the right one is in front nearer your feet, and do the same movement slowly. How is it different to you? Think of your shoulders, and chest, and sternum. What about the clavicles? What about the shoulder blades? Now notice what changes as soon as she has the movement in mind; even the eyes are in a different place.

You know, a person's eyes normally go to the horizon and when they are not there, the person is preoccupied. Something disturbs his attention, his vision, and this is a sign that the person may be experiencing pain. Now put both hands behind you and do this same little movement, as tiny as you can. Open your knees whether you want to or not, but don't press them to open. Now change over the legs, slowly. Can you see? She has a very good nervous system, but talking blocks thinking. Alright, now, turn the right hand over to the left and see whether you can bring your feet a little bit nearer to yourselves with your hands. Now take both hands to the side, see whether you can get up to the left. For a painful back it's bloody marvelous. Now is it a little painful? No, that's all we can do. You can see by the amount of the opening of your knees that the tension of the back is less. (Answer: "Yes, it is going.")

If you sit there and you do something in the same spirit another time—you will see that the pain is gone.

In order to improve in a reasonable time I use my hands to direct the person to the kind of sensory response we are looking for. When a person is in real pain for years, he doesn't believe change is possible. Such a person interferes with himself and does not move the way you do. Therefore, he can not improve, unless I do it with him. I think of it as dancing, and in dancing I can make a person walk with me. That is what we call functional integration.

We have spent an hour and it is good to stop, walk around, so that we can continue with a fresh attitude. See if you can remember now what I did? Just before you walk out think what are the new things that you have learned, and not just the new things that you can write down on paper. By the way, I advise you to recall what you want to remember and write this down carefully and thoughtfully later in your room. That way, you will write down what you know. Otherwise, if you write here and it's written quickly in a kind of shorthand, when you will read it next time, you will read into it things that we haven't said. In an hour's time you wouldn't know what it means. Therefore, to take notes means to be wired in a scholastic learning and exercising and not using your brain, not using your thinking ability. Learning this other way will make you a little bit better—you as you are—in a way you want to be; a little bit of your dreams will become realized. When you take notes, you stop yourselves from evolving the way you want.

Alright, now think a minute of what we have learned that was striking to you, that was new to you. There were some very important things—the question of the center of gravity, the question of what is the better movement, that the pelvis must make a continuous curve, that whatever the movement, it can stop at any moment or continue in its trajectory, or go back in the same trajectory, that it is immaterial how fat you are, or ugly you are, or beautiful, or old or young, decrepit or healthy. When the nervous system and the brain work the way we have just done, you spread the gospel throughout your system. (laughter) Well, let's have some coffee. Thank you. (applause)

Can everybody say what sort of improvement could be made with the lessons up to now? Has anybody something which he did not like, the way, the length, the details, the voice or whatever? Anything where you could say, 'If it were like that I would be really satisfied?' Does anybody have an objection? (Answer: 'This seems trivial to me, but I would like to be able to start facing and end up the same way. It seems awkward to me that if I want to sit down to face you I have to face back. Is there a way to make a more complete turn? You ask what we find. That to me would make it more perfect, if I could turn more or something so that I could face the same direction.') Now, anybody else? (Answer: 'I find it more difficult to turn towards the right than the left. My natural inclination is still to turn towards the left and it is still a thing I do not understand.') Well, that is not my fault. (laughter) I am not joking. You see the problem of our terminology, that worthless terminology, that is used the world over. Now, can anybody express in a few words the purpose of the lesson? (replies) Why are we doing it? Don't talk, just think, a minute at least, and then say. The thing in itself maybe was pleasant enough, nice, but we are going to do five days, and there must be some sense in what we are doing, as we always do something with a purpose. But this is an error. When you get to the purpose, what happens? You have nothing more to do. It's the way to the purpose that's important; for instance we all have one purpose —to die. Everyone will reach that purpose. The difference between being born and dying is only in the way we get from one to the other. Therefore, the way of reaching the purpose is the important thing, and not the purpose. The purpose is secondary; and once you achieve a purpose, have you then finished your life? You get the Nobel Prize, you can go to sleep, and die. You won a million dollars, finished. Surely it sounds crazy. Those who are present here—there are probably not two who had the same purpose in coming here. Therefore, it's the way you got here that's important.

I cannot help using words like everybody else, otherwise, we cannot do anything—with each other. But you see, I don't mean the purpose, as you would understand it normally. I mean that life must be improved. The way we get to the purpose must be improved. Therefore if we did the lesson like that, just to improve the way we get up and down; that is only a minor thing. You have lived to now—doing the movement the way you did. And you didn't feel that your life was spoiled through that. Therefore, what we learned was something really for some other purpose. That purpose was to improve all action. Action is something which does not exist by itself; there is no action without feeling, without sensing, without thinking, therefore, improved action will improve our life; that means feeling, sensing, thinking and acting will improve. There is nothing more to do anyway. What we did is an example of action and the way we set out about action, how we organize ourselves to act. Why was the final result better? We found that it was more intentional, that we can stop and start —but surely you are not sitting and getting up in order to find out you can stop, and go back, and do something else. How come that this is a better way of getting up than another one? One commentator is dissatisfied with the way she turned the other way round, and did not get up in the position which we faced.

Now, the point is that most human action—as it is for other animals—has a pattern which is unique to each person. When a group of substances, gets a boundary—in our case the skin —it separates that matter from the rest of the world. This is individualization; there is the person and the world outside. The boundary separates you from the rest of the world, it separates me from the rest of the world, and makes an outside world and me. Now, the boundary creates the situation that the outside world and myself are actually the same thing; because the piece of matter that is the boundary cannot exist by itself, it must gain a means of acting, thinking, moving, sensing. And to produce activity, it must have energy, which can only come from the outside. We take air, water, food, and we reject what is useless. Now, all these things pass through the boundary; therefore individualization means separating the world into an individual and an outside world, and the relation between that individual matter and the rest of the matter, the piece of matter in the boundary and the rest of the matter, involves continuous interchange. If that interchange between the incoming and the outgoing matter is interfered within its continuity and its simplicity, then there is illness either in the world or in the person, or in both.

When we learn something, in the way I am speaking, we have to learn something which improves the relation of the individual to the rest of the world and to himself. And one of the most important things in the living thing is what? What is the difference between a living thing which is growing, and just vegetation which is also life? Vegetation has heredity, it has consistency. A given fruit, a given tree, will never produce other fruit, and therefore the seeds will produce the same tree and the same fruit. It has DNA; it has all the constituents, but it has no movement. It's passive. It has self-reproduction; it

has self-maintenance. It has the interchange of matter that is
a necessity for all living things from a bacteria or to you,
yourself. But animal life has self-preservation. This has great
implications in regards to movement, for the most drastic test
of movement is self-preservation. Why, for example, from the
point of view of self-preservation—did we get up? Normally an
animal would not get up unless it heard, or saw, or smelled,
or felt a change in the environment which it could not inter-
pret as being safe. Think of how a dog lies with perked ear
looking around. What change in the environment may com-
promise its safety, its self-preservation? Now the movements
that we do, all the movements, are initially, fundamentally
made like that. Think of human beings, 10,000 years ago.
What were the signals that made them get up, and why would
it be important for them to get up smoothly and quickly so
that they can do it without preliminary rearrangement? Why
didn't I like the way you did it before? Because you made two
or three movements in place of one. If there were a cobra
behind you within a yard you would be killed. But in the new
movement you learned you can get up on your feet immediately. It has that disadvantage that you turned your face the
other way. But that is the point. Suppose someone there wants
to put a knife in your back. Now, if you try to get up to avoid
that knife in any better way than to turn as we did, what
would happen? (laughter)—come on; try it; stick the knife.

[Some people in the group demonstrate. Moshe asks the
victim] Why did you do that? (Answer: "Because there is a
knife coming!") Therefore this is the movement for self-preservation. When you sit and you are quiet, and you hear a noise
from behind, you are turned in the direction of the danger and
ready for action in one movement. In actual self-preservation
you are too late if you make two movements and then respond.

[To one of the audience] Go and try to strangle her from
behind. (laughter) Now, look what you're doing, you're using
the principle we just learned. You'll find that your system is
cleverer than you; your system is now aware that this is the
right thing to do. Now, what's the answer? Is that the best way

to do it? If you turn your back to me you can only run away, but that too can be also a good thing. It depends on the distance of the attacker. If the danger is far away, you can turn your back and run away. But if it's too late, you need to be ready quickly. Therefore you see that the question of good movement is primarily whether it assures your survival and self-preservation, and for that it is important to attend to propulsion. Now, we don't do that because in our way of life, in our culture, self-preservation is supposed to be assured by the police. Many people who are mugged are killed do not think of doing what we have learned, and they don't know how to run away. The self-preservation is compromised, and the movement is poorly done. Suppose you decided tomorrow you are going to hold up an Alsatian dog in San Francisco, to buy drugs. If I give you a spear, I bet you one in a hundred that you don't succeed in spearing the dog. What will happen? How does the dog avoid the attack? I tried; I have photographs of my attempts and I failed. The dog will stand there. He won't run away. But as you thrust your spear the dog will move just slightly and your spear will hit air.

Now, that's the answer to you. We examine movement from the point of view of self-preservation, and find that the quality of the movement has special ingredients, particularly that there is no preliminary reorganization. Then any movement which has one preliminary change and a second and a third, is a bad movement.

Our nervous system is constructed to make self-preservation possible, and continuous movement easy. But if you don't have this fundamental thing right, then whatever you learn afterwards is just piling up mistake on mistake, until you live 40 years, and say my posture is bad. But what do you mean by that? Why is a posture bad, and what is posture in general? Why is it bad if I hang my head like that? Is it bad because aesthetically it doesn't satisfy you? Well, it doesn't make any difference to me whether you like me or not. I'm already too old anyway to be liked. Well, so what's bad in this posture? If I wanted to jump or go to a tree, I can't. I must do a preliminary reorganization. Therefore, the ingredient of good posture is the one that you have learned in doing this movement, that allows you to be direct, swift, efficient and harmoniously satisfactory to yourself. But there is something I have already insisted on without saying. If you move your pelvis, your arms and legs organize themselves to do just the thing that you need. Our heredity is common, and the experience of our ancestors is common. The body is constructed so that the powerful part, in which all the strong muscles work, and carry your weight, is the pelvis. The muscles with the biggest cross section including the gluteals, the quadriceps, the psoas, the stomach and lateral muscles, are around the pelvis, and therefore the hands and legs only transmit that power to the place where you need it.

[Moshe directs a person to improve the movement in front of the group.] Watch when you get up. Remember what I told you—that again is faulty. Look, there your thumb interferes. Put the thumb there and see how much power you have got. Can you see that the minutest detail of your movement becomes of paramount importance when you look at it from the point of view of how movement was introduced in the human species? It was introduced to preserve us. If our ancestors were not preserved, we wouldn't exist. Those who didn't have the right movement, those who placed the thumb in danger died, they were not reproduced as well as those who didn't. Darwin suggested that. The funny thing is that survival is not accomplished by learning the right thing to do, but avoiding the thing that compromises your vitality, your life. Survival is a negative thing; the species that survive are those who avoided destruction. No one is omniscient. The brontasaurus died not because he knew how the temperature would change. He avoided temperatures that killed him. And then he moved to new places, but died because the temperature changed and he wasn't fit. Those that survive are those who have avoided the destructive power through mutation. We know that now, and not because they said: "Ah, there will be atomic energy, that's why we'll survive." There's no animal in the world that can say what it has to do in order to be on earth in another thousand years. I'll give you an example, a very fine example. Prof. Hamburger, a French surgeon, wrote a very, very interesting book in which he talks about the survival of Darwinian ideas. Prof. Hamburger is originally an Algerian Jew, who knew the Sahara, and Africa. He discovered a funny sort of thing. You know malaria is a deadly disease, which kills many African people. There is also an extraordinary disease, a fatal heart disease, which is also very destructive, because usually people die by the age of 6–7. But those who survive this disease and grow up do not need to be innoculated against malaria. They are free of tropical malaria. Everyone else gets malaria, but these people get bitten by the mosquitoes and nothing happens. Now, Prof. Hamburger suggested this. We don't know who the humans are that will survive in a 100 years, 200 years. He says, suppose that there is severe malaria, and DDT no longer stops its spread. Many people die of malaria again. You have to do something else about it. But it could happen that the people who survive are those that have a hereditary fault in their hearts. Those would be the future humanity. In other words, we don't know who'll survive. You can see that that's a possibility.

Now just to show you again, that movement, from the survival point of view, dictates that you don't put the thumb in jeopardy because that makes your movement slow. Why does it make it slow? Because our nervous system knows that if you put your full weight on your thumb it will break. Therefore this is a non-vital habit, and a bad one. And by the way, if you look at people who know what fighting is, they will never endanger themselves by putting their thumb out in space where it can be broken. A small detail, but if you want to be yourself as you dream, you have to take out the rubbish that you have learned which is not yours. You've learned it by imitating others, by finding it from people who have never had to protect themselves from being mugged, or from being in war. We must make a completely different attitude towards life.

Now, peace is also impossible unless people know that. When people can stand on their own and are not afraid, they can be friendly to each other. That's why a grownup person is never afraid of a child, and he'll never hurt the child normally, unless he is a bit deranged. If a child hits you, or pinches you, will you kill him? Would you throw him out of the window? What will you do because his power and his ability does not threaten your self-preservation? Therefore weak people do wicked things such as make war. Those who are strong enough, not afraid. Alright, now let's go on further with understanding movement. We can find out many things that are impossible to solve, otherwise. What, for example, is a good posture? A good posture is the one from which one can move in any direction. If I walk like so, [Moshe demonstrates] you would think I have a hernia. It is a bad posture because to go forward I must stop walking like that. I must either go on that leg so that I can walk forward, or on this leg, otherwise I cannot lift the leg, therefore standing on both legs, all the time like that, is a bad posture, for moving. But for fighting many people think it's good. Wrestlers will start with this posture because they know that nobody will attack them from behind, and only need to go forward. But if one was attacked from both front and behind, one would be dead before one started. So we return to the idea that we can undertake any movement, from 16 different directions; up and down, right, left, forward and back, without any preliminary movement.

Now can you see it's a funny way of looking at things when you suddenly begin to realize that there is a way of conducting oneself so that you feel yourself growing in your own way, by just appreciating what movement is, what it means, how it grew in the human species? That's what we learned this morning: to do a movement so that there is *one movement*—down and up. Now you will find something extraordinary. Get up. Do the movement we learned this morning and go as fast as you can. Do it about ten times. Change over your hands. Can you measure the speed of the movement like that? How long did it take you to do the ten movements; less than half a minute? I say, look, how your hearts beat; are you out of breath? Are you really tired? Put your hands there and get up in any other way but the way you just learned. Do that ten times, but fast, and you'll see what that does to you. (Laughter) By the time you get up twice it's already what you did ten times before. Stop and see, that's how a doctor measures your heart fatigue and the time it is necessary to recover. The way we did it before can be done a hundred times and you'll not be out of breath, and a 100 you'll do in a tenth of the time of any other way.

Another important thing we learned is that the movement must initiate from the pelvis, not the hand, nor foot, but the *direction* of the movement is given by the movement of the head. You remember you did not look up, nor down. Therefore your head remained unconcerned with the movement. Try it out. Do any other movement and you'll find that you cannot move the head right and left continuously. Now you'll find that once you learn the content of what we did, you can do it in any other way without having the whole too, and that is real learning of free choice. Once you learn the real essence of the movement, you can do it without the hands, with the wrong hand, with the wrong leg; it doesn't matter. But the ability of your head to remain mobile while you move is essential for self-preservation. Now you'll understand some funny things that you've been sensing all your life but you could not understand.

For example, lions and tigers as well as other animals stand on one leg and move their heads. Now in our movement, if I wish to get up, it is difficult, if my head is stiff.

Movements were first invented by nature for self-preservation. You'll see that there's no animal who does anything without keeping the head mobile. A cat after a mouse sits there, and twiddles his eyes, the tiger watches to get an animal, but his head keeps on turning. If he doesn't, the gorilla with a branch can open his head with one strike. A zebra may stay within ten or fifteen feet of a lion and feed, but you'll see that during the feeding his head is mobile, and he listens, and turns the eyes and you can see it's enough for the lion to move his tail and the zebra—fast—is away. No animal fixes the head and if you don't fix your head, you can get up swiftly and easily as you did and can do any bloody thing. In fact, if your head is mobile, you don't even have to fix your legs. You don't have to stop in the middle. You've learned that without knowing it because you did one movement correctly, with your head free and your power originating in your pelvis. And when one fixes one's head while the pelvis is unable to carry out the action, then one cannot do anything.

It is your head that you use to relate yourself to the environment, to find out how you can preserve yourself. And of course when you have that, it's enough to see that the pelvis initiates. I get up in that way—look—ready either to attack or to disappear. [Moshe demonstrates standing from his chair effortlessly.] Now this is the ingredient of good movement, and this is the essence of a good posture, and these things must be learned in the body. When you give the body one taste, you learn it better than with a thousand explanations.

LESSON TWO:
THINKING AND DOING

Will you please lie on your back. Spread your legs a bit wider, wider than your shoulders, but not very much; put both hands on either side of the body with the palms downwards, and the elbows therefore wider than your body. Would you close your eyes, and imagine that you are going to use your left leg only and that your face, nose, and head will turn so that you stand on the left leg; that means the rest of the body, your eyes, your nose, your head are comfortable and standing on the left leg. Therefore your eyes look to your left foot and the back of your head is in such a situation, that you won't make any intention and it will turn by itself, so the left leg carries your weight. Now very, very slowly flex and straighten your left foot, so that you don't make any jerky movements with your knee or hip. But let your head move in such a way that you can stand on the left leg, and see your left side. The outside of the left foot and the right side of the left foot and your hip joint and the spine and the shoulders are so organized that you won't make any intentional movement of your head; you will just imagine. Don't turn your foot right and left but only flex it and straighten it in the tiniest amount possible. Now very, very slowly, make a tiny little movement to lift your left knee off the floor. Make it so imperceptible that you feel only your heel on the floor wanting to move. Now in your imagination lift your left knee and put it back where it was; the heel comes near to you, because your leg shortens. When you put it back, the heel goes away, and therefore the foot must fit the movement of the heel.

Think again of lifting your left knee, and as your heel comes near to you, does your foot flex or straighten? Continue that movement and at the same time as you lift your knee, press your left hip to the floor. When you straighten your leg, lift your left hip off the floor. Observe yourself; where do you imagine that your hip joint is? Is it the outside? Is it the top of the femur, the grand trochanter, the point that you could touch with your hand on the left side? Or is it actually the head of the femur, the part that moves in the socket of your pelvis. Now while you do that, can you find where the socket is on the inside of your left thigh? Can you feel it? Can you locate it at the back of your pelvis, between your legs, anus, the bones on which you sit, and the grand trochanter, which is a good four inches away from the hip joint.

Now keep lifting your knee, arching the heel nearer and stretch your leg and lift your hip joint in the smallest possible movement, so that you don't see anything outside. Then flex the knee and put the hip joint down; you also lift both shoulders and the sternum or breast bone, between the two clavicles, or collar bones. Let your head remain lying on the floor. But, of course, if you lift both shoulders and the middle of the sternum and flex your knee, your hip joint sticks to the floor and your spine does something. As you continue, feel what happens in the back of your head. When you lift both shoulders, both clavicles and the sternum and see your stomach, are the small floating ribs pulled inwards, or not? Do you feel your body lengthening or shortening? Is the middle of your spine pressed to the floor, or is it staying long? Now slowly increase the movement of your shoulders and knee so that anybody who is carefully watching you could tell what was in your imagination. Do you press both elbows to the floor? Is your head being left in the middle, or is the nose to the left or the right? Which part of your head remains on the floor? Now keep the same thought, and you can see that when you straighten your knee, you lift the hip joints, the shoulders go back and then the other way around again. Increase the velocity, and keep on making it faster and smaller, until you can do it really fast. Do it at least 50 times like that—fast. Your knee should not go sideways.

Would you make the movement with less force, and as fast as your imagination can do it, and stop a second, then make it faster. Who senses that fastness? Do you actually lift your shoulders? Is the chest in the middle? Do you contract your stomach muscles? Do you draw your stomach in, when you lift your shoulders? Now stop moving your leg in your imagination, and just move your stomach in, and lift your shoulders, and reverse pushing your stomach out and shoulders down. Is that what you did before? Do you feel the lower ribs in front of you, and behind you, on either side of the chest? Now do the same thing with your leg and hip joint and instead of your shoulders think of lifting your head. Do you grow taller? Or do you flex your stomach? Where do you bend to sit up? Now lift your knee once, and heel, and leg as you did before, and lift your shoulders as if your shoulders are going to see your knee from the middle of your sternum. The next movement you'll do the same thing trying to kiss your knee as it comes towards your face and this time you will lift your head to meet your knee. Now, make those movements barely perceptible, but increase the speed a bit and do two movements with your shoulders and two movements with your head. Observe the difference in feeling, in sensation, and observe if you actually lie on the left hip joint more clearly than on the right, and that your chest and back of the rib cage actually not in the middle.

Now make the movement slightly more pronounced and do the whole flexion movement, from the sole of your foot to the tip of your head, doing two movements with the head, then two movements with the shoulders only. Stop and lie still. Note what it feels like lying like that. Lift both hands to the ceiling, interlace your fingers, and make a circle with both arms. That means you will bend your elbows so that it feels like you have made a circle. Keep on flexing your legs, head, shoulders, and knee, with the idea that your head goes through that circle, and your knee comes to join your mouth at some point. Make the movement so it is barely perceptible.

Note only the difference of the pressure in your left hip and your right hip and your shoulder blades. Now bend your right leg, stand on your right foot, and continue to flex the whole body any way you like, without any restriction of your shoulders or head, and imagine that you bring your left knee to touch your face. Do as little as possible, so that one who's eager to know what you're thinking could see it, but you should not do it so that anybody from a mile could say what you're doing. Again, observe what you do with your chest, your stomach, the small of the back, your pelvis, your shoulder blades, the pectoral muscles, the ribs. While you think, slowly eliminate everything in your imagination except your right shoulder and your left hip joint; continue the movement, but your left hip joint and right shoulder go towards one another, and go apart. Now, change the pattern and move your right shoulder—and left hip alternately to the floor rather than together. Now stretch your right leg and keep on doing the movement with your hip joint and shoulder alternately.

Lower your hands and continue. Note only what happens in the spine and the ribs on the floor. Now keep flexing the left leg and the shoulders—gently without moving your head. Move your left knee upwards and the hip joint downward so that you can feel a slight movement—a sliding of the heel on the floor, and direct your right shoulder and your chest, so that if you were to get up your left leg would be in the middle, and your face would follow the line from the heel to your head. It means your left heel, knee, and hip joint, your spine, sternum, middle of the chest, middle of the back, is *just* in the middle of the direction of the face, and therefore your head is directed down the line to your left heel. Now bend your left knee, put your left foot on the floor, and this time gently lift the left hip as you push the floor with your left foot. Again make the movement imperceptible so you can trace the line of movement to your right shoulder. Does your right shoulder blade lie flatter on the floor? Does your spine increase in length? And now, with each imaginary push of the hip joint upwards, can you feel what happens on the left side of your chest? What is different from the movement of the ribs on the right? And when your hip leaves the floor does your right shoulder lift or slide higher? Now do both. Make the movement so that when you push your foot, your hip lifts and the chest rocks and the small ribs come forward so your right shoulder blade is actually stretched on the floor and pushed to lie flatter. The next thought is this, once you push your left hip think of your shoulder lifting with the clavicle, and moving towards your left hip joint. Do it several times. Note now what you do with your eyes; do they look to either side of the knee, or foot? Are they looking to infinity, or at one part of your body? Are they looking downward? Think of your mouth, and tongue. Can you now make the whole movement with your breath as shallow as possible, breathing as if you were asleep, that is, not bothering about it all?

Stretch out, and slowly move your right leg to the left to close the gap between your legs. And now very, very slowly, move both legs imperceptibly more to the left. Bring them back to the normal, and then take them a little bit more to the left, and back. And now you'll feel that every time you think of moving the legs, you'll find your head thinks also and moves in the same direction. Now several times; think of it and observe only what you do with the middle part of yourselves— between the shoulders, the chest and spine in the back, hip joints, and pelvis as you imagine yourself going to the left with the legs and the head. And now, very slowly, think without doing it; you're taking your legs and head to the right and again to the left. Now think several times and actually make a tiny little movement after you've been through it mentally. Take both legs a little bit more to the left, a tenth of an inch, and then another tenth of an inch to the right. Increase, very, very gradually, the movement of your heels—on the floor— with your legs as nearly straight as you can make them. They must bend a little, otherwise there's friction. As you go to the left, see how much your head has moved. Keep your breathing shallow. Now reduce the effort to make it so close to your imagination that there is nothing to see, and keep on increasing the movement to the left and to the right instead of a tenth of an inch two tenths of an inch. Observe what you're doing with your chest and think, when you begin to do it really that it's different from what you imagined before. Continue increasing the movement of the legs to the left and to the right, and find out; how do you lift your legs to move to the left, and to the right? Increase the movement to the right with both legs, very gradually, and note that as soon as you have the legs moving, no matter how little to the right really, your head and face have already turned to the right. Continue it, moving slowly to the left effortlessly and slowly to the right; the middle of your body will do more movement, but you should not direct it. If you direct it, then there'll be no important change in your normal way of doing it, and the lesson is wasted.

Now, gradually increase the movement of your legs and head, and see what happens to your chest, spine, pelvis, mouth. The movement should become more and more the expression of your own rhythm, your own relation of your legs to your chest and head. Remember, it's not important for you to move at all. Your legs and heels, we said, were together. And we started by making the right leg touch the left. Now keep on making the movement larger, but so gradually that you feel no compulsion to succeed in going to the right, or to the left. Note only how different the movement to the left is from the movement to the right, because when we did it to the left, we did a lot of thinking; to the right we didn't. Continue, effortlessly, doing nothing, leaving the rest of the body as silent as necessary, the breath shallow. You have no intention of succeeding. Increase the movement until you can feel, if somebody looked, he would see that you are doing the same thing right and left.

Observe; do you feel as you bend to the left, or to the right, that you are getting taller? Or smaller? And what happens to your chest? Which part lifts? When you start from the right, which part moves when you think of moving to the left? Some parts get closer to the floor and some more away from it. As you pay attention, which parts actually produce these movements? Continue until you feel that you've passed the middle, and that you are actually making the movement to the right, and the left, the same amount. Now when you do that can you feel that your elbows move? How do your hands move? And what do the shoulders do? And then what about the 7th cervical vertebra? That's the large vertebra in the middle of the shoulders just below your neck, that sticks out in between the shoulders.

Now move your right leg away from the left and go back to the movements where you bend your left knee, and move your left heel, flexing your foot. Repeat the movements we did before using both shoulders and your face, bending your knee and keeping your left hip joint to the floor as you flex. Lift your right shoulder and head, and see what you're doing with your elbows. And now increase the movement gradually as if you were to actually do it, and sit up on the left side of your body. Now think that you're going to sit up, but don't do it, but continue thinking that you're sitting up, flexing your leg and shoulders and head. You will find there are two ways of sitting up: one is that you lengthen and your shoulders lift enough to carry your head behind. The other is that you flatten your chest as you lift your head. Try both ways, and realize which fits you better. Now, slowly roll to the side, any side you wish, and get up. Walk around, observe how you feel, whether you're taller, or smaller. How are you breathing? Look at each other's faces. Can you tell by looking at the face which side was the one we worked on in our imagination? Which eye is bigger? Which side of the face is longer? On which leg do you feel you stand more easily? Where are your shoulders? What's the difference between standing on the left foot while walking and on the right? Now stand like that, and keep on turning around yourselves to the right. Just observe how that feels. Now very slowly turn around yourself to the left and notice whether you feel a difference in the quality of the turning. Now let's have a minute rest.

LESSON THREE:
EXPLORING THE FLOOR: THE MOVEMENTS OF THE SHOULDER

Lie on your stomach, and bend your right leg on the floor, with your knee to your right. Turn your head to the right. Your left arm lies along your side with the palm facing the ceiling. Your right hand is near to your face. Now, just slowly, think of how you would move your right hand on the floor as it is, just a little bit to the right, a little bit to the left. Observe that movement is easy. Now move your right hand a little bit upwards; is it more difficult? Upwards means in the direction of your head.

Now explore the floor with your right hand, but gently, make very small movements, upwards, downwards, right, left. Just observe, in which direction does your hand move more easily? Don't try to make the exploration large enough to reach Africa; just make a small movement, the smallest movement which feels—like it's really nothing, effortless. It's important to find the differences. Which side is easier—is it to the right, to the left, up or down? You'll find one direction is difficult, and this difficulty is only relieved if you do something with your elbow.

Now observe which position and which direction is the most difficult. Find how your elbow can help you. Some of you have done it already spontaneously, because everything I teach is an organization which is proper to our nervous system. Therefore there are some people who will do it right from the start before I tell them. Their mistake is doing the right thing. What do you think of that? Now when, I say, lift the elbow, or help with the elbow, which direction do I mean? Many people have already made the right mistake, and some the wrong mistake. How can you lift your elbow without doing something with your other shoulder, and your head, and your pelvis? Don't lift, go slower, so that you can organize yourself to your action by making a fundamental change in yourself. If you go fast you don't allow it. Learning must be made so slow, that in everybody's makeup, activity can be organized. When you are well organized you can go fast. We can go then as fast as we did today in the twisting movement to stand. If you remember I told you to go faster, to show you that if we go faster we are wrong, and ruin ourselves. You ruin your joints, brain and your breathing by going fast when learning a new choice; and thus make it impossible to succeed. Now would you please leave your hand where it is and just move your right elbow up from the floor. Your hand should flex and stay on the floor.

Now lift your elbow, and you'll see that your elbow does not want to move unless you do something with your hand so that it's comfortable, and if you go fast, you won't notice what you actually did with your shoulder blade, and your clavicle, and you think you did the movement with the elbow. Continue moving your hand in conjunction with the movement of raising and lowering your elbow to the floor. Your elbow can't move without the clavicle. It should be part of your awareness, and not just an automatic activity. Lift your elbow as if it's lifting towards the ceiling, and stop when the quality of movement changes. Then you'll find that the quality of movement becomes poor in your wrist and hand, as well as in your shoulder, and, so, the clavicle. If your shoulder is difficult to move, move it upwards towards your right ear. Then move slowly and not so fast that your head moves also. The faster you go the less you will change in the direction which is necessary for you. Feel the position where your elbow becomes more difficult to move than the initial movement. When that is clear, stop moving.

If you ever had to play two and a half hours on a fiddle with a bow or on the cello, you would find out how the hand needs to moves. Have you seen Casals at the age of 90 play the cello? Did you notice that movement in his hand? You won't get it if you make this movement fast. Yet Casals got there by himself. Now very slowly, lift your elbow to the point where you feel it's getting more difficult. Try at this point to lift the wrist from the floor without changing the position of your elbow. Lift the lowest part of the wrist off the floor first, and then lift your fingers, with the wrist down, and you'll find out how much useless tension there is in your hand which makes your shoulder difficult to move. Do a few movements with your wrist and your hand, and then lift your thumb by turning your hand, so that you lean on the small finger and the other way round. As you continue, sense what's happening in your right leg and the left shoulder, and left leg. Now leave your elbow on the floor, and explore with your right hand the same area as you did before. Observe for yourself how you dare to go to Nigeria and to Victoria Falls, all sorts of places where you couldn't move before. That is wonderful learning.

Now stop somewhere in one direction, or the other where you feel—ah, the quality of my movement is different here. At that point move your elbow a little bit to the right and a little bit to the left; now watch, how do you make that movement? Obviously you can't lift your elbow without doing something in your shoulder. Observe what the other shoulder does. See now whether you can move your hand to explore the part of the floor near your forehead, moving of course everything that is necessary for that. Notice the quality of the movement and stop when the quality of the movement changes. Your intention should be to go around your head, on the floor. What do you have to do with your elbow and shoulder in order to improve? Make your hand come over the right side of your head, near the ear, but just above. Touch your head, not from above —but by taking your hand along the floor around your head, until you can touch the parietal side, the right side. The parietal part is the section of your head from the temple to the ear on the highest part of the head. As you move your hand there, see what you have to do with your elbow in order to make the movement as good as you have done up to now. Then slide the fingers of your right hand to your right ear, behind your right ear on the back of your head. Move down, along your neck, and find what you have to do with your elbow that you didn't do up to now. How would you slide your hand down along your neck in between your shoulder blades?

You must be able to move your shoulder in conjunction with your elbow or your hand will never get there. Now you'll see your elbow needs to lift to the height of your head, in fact higher. Direct your fingers wherever you like downwards on your back until you can feel your neck and the vertebrae, between the shoulders. As you continue, observe that when your elbow goes up like that, some part of yourself softens and gets pressed to the floor. If this doesn't happen, you will only have pain in your shoulder, or neck, or somewhere else. Now stop it; come back.

Would you please explore the floor with your right hand again and see what are the new regions where your hand goes with great, great comfort. Observe there are places you can reach where you had no intention of going at all previously. Now see whether you could go also to the right, without stretching your hand to the right. Move your hand on the floor from the right towards yourself and notice what you have to do with your elbow and shoulder so that you can touch your chest with your hand. Touch somewhere near your breast, below your breast, anywhere on the lower ribs, anywhere, where it's really comfortable. How can you make it comfortable? Now would you please explore your chest from the lower ribs upwards until you can go as high as possible effortlessly, with the same quality of movement and find at which point you lose this quality. Touch your chest on the side not in front. Don't lift your breast in the air. Can you see your hand will never come under your armpit? Now someone has immediately tried to go under the armpit in a different way as soon as I said that. Such people are very good, but are a pain in the neck to themselves and to others. Now slowly, move your hand along the side of your chest. This time when you come to the point where it's difficult to touch, please turn your fingers inwards so that you touch your chest with the back of your nails and the back of your hand. [Some members of the group did not follow this instruction.]

If we don't have a language to communicate, it's impossible for you to learn properly. You still need a whip. Now as you need a whip and I haven't got the time to whip you, and I haven't got a whip, would you watch me for a second? There's only one method for people who can't learn, which is to show them with an example, so that they can do it. Now look. I am taking my hand around my chest, but I can't go on. Then I turn my hand so that the fingers, the back of the fingers, and the nails touch my side. Then I find I can go where I didn't before, and that was what I asked you to do. Go where you feel you can't go anymore, don't break your back. You need to change, or you'll never get your hand where it can go. But in order to change you'll find that if you do what I suggest, whether you want it or not, your shoulder changes and your chest moves. One did it, and got under her armpit immediately, and all the others who wouldn't follow the idea couldn't move to that point if they killed themselves.

[Moshe now demonstrates taking his hand under his armpit where it's difficult and turning his hand.] Now that's the simple thing, move to the place where it's difficult, that's here for me; it's here. Then watch what I do, just that. Look, turn, notice what the wrist does, what the chest does, look what the shoulder does, and when you do that you find—oh, funny, why was it difficult before? It isn't difficult at all. It's only that my brain is stiff: Now, that's an example. Imitate me now, and you won't learn anything. Slowly go along the chest and to any point that is difficult. Do the kind of movement that you saw me doing, but slowly. Don't move right or left, only that movement, and back. You'll see, astonishing as it may be, if you do three movements at the same spot, it appears that your hand moves there in a way that would not be possible otherwise. Then go along the chest, and at each point move where you can reach with your hand easily, and then twist your wrist and so that you can move to the more difficult spot. You will find yourself astonishingly reaching at places which were unthinkable.

Now observe only what happens to your shoulders, and put your hand on the floor and explore the floor and see how different it is, then touch the lowest part of the small ribs with the palm of your hand. At that moment turn your wrist so that the nails glide on the back and then see whether you can direct your hand slowly, gently, a little bit at a time, with the back of your hand touching the lower ribs, in the direction of your head along the spine. If you find that you can't, just bend the wrist, and touch the tips of the fingers to the spine. At this point make a movement in the wrist, and take the hand back where it was, and lift your wrist off your back, and go back, with just the wrist. Then lift your fingers off your back by closing your hand, and touch with the fingers, and leave the wrist and do that three or four times. Notice whether you now make tremendous efforts that are futile. See whether you can lower your elbow and turn the nails on your back. Move your head to the left side if necessary. Now slide your hand on your back on the left side and see whether you can turn the fingers in the direction of your head—a little bit, not much, and back again and a little bit, and find out what you have to do with your elbow and your shoulder blade and your chest, in order to slide the backs of the fingers, the back of the hands, along the small ribs of the left side. Go as much to the left as is easy, and as far upwards as is easy, in the direction of your fingers. This time close your hand and then lift your wrist, leaning on your knuckles. Stay there and see that the tip of your right shoulder goes up to your nose and back. Open your hand, and explore the left side of your chest with the back of the hand and observe: you go places where you couldn't go before and you may even bring your nails to go in the direction of your neck along your spine. Notice what your shoulders and your elbow do. Let your hand down again with your hand on the floor in front of you. Just explore the floor and see which points are now within your immediate, simple, easy grasp, which weren't before. Check for the quality of the movement and notice this extraordinary thing: although you can go further and better, up and down, and any way you like, touch your chest, and touch the back of your hand so that the fingertips can go directly under the armpit—you will find suddenly that if you can do that, you can place your palm against your ribs and have your fingertips touch the armpit. Before you learned just now, it was not possible since your brain didn't know how to organize the relative parts to do it, and the ideas that came first to your mind did not work. All you could do was to strain and break something; now it is easy.

Bring your hand to the floor over your head as you did before, and slide it above your head, behind your head, and just see where your hand goes now. Can you go between your shoulders? Can it move from the right shoulder blade to the left shoulder blade with ease? The tips of your fingers move also to the right and to the left. Now there's only one way, your elbow must lift if the shoulder blades are to be touched in the same way. Observe how your hand lies on your spine, and your fingertips point to the left. Move the fingertips to the right from one shoulder blade to the other. Your elbows must move in the opposite direction, otherwise it won't work. Now slide your hand from one shoulder blade to the other, or more or less left and right and turn your wrist so that the fingertips turn left.

If you can't move the fingertips, make your hand into a fist, and put your wrist lower, and the elbow higher, so that the inside of the wrist is touching your body and then lift it again. Lift your wrist, and then find out what two movements like that can accomplish for the movement of your hand. You're gaining an inch or two just by thinking it. Now would you please move your hand from above your head down to the floor, with the palm downwards, and stretch the palm above your head as far as it will go effortlessly with the palm upwards. Where will it go? Don't go to places where the quality of the movement changes; but if it changes, find out what you could do to make the quality the same. In other words—why can't you touch the floor with the back of your thumb? You'll see that that has to do with how you move your shoulder blade and your elbow. Bring it near to you and the thumb will lie easily. Now go upwards and see: where would you have to move your shoulder and your head, without turning it the other way? What will you have to do with yourself to be able to touch with your thumb? If it worked by straining, you would have done it already. Now put the back of your hand with your fingers upwards, your nails towards your head, palm upwards, and then do something with the rest of your body. Your left hand should lie with the palm upwards behind you. Adjust the right side of yourselves so you can go upwards without change. Avoid that strain; change your body in such a way that there's no strain.

You'll always find in a big group, a few people will do it with the greatest ease; one has done it already. You'll find that unless the lower part of the shoulder blade can lift in the air, you won't do it. Don't put restrictions on yourselves that stop the shoulder blade. Anyway, stop it a minute, except you in front of me.

[Moshe has person demonstrate for the group.] Bring your elbow back and notice what happens to the shoulder blades. Now do the movement. You know why the others didn't do it? Notice what she does with her shoulder blade. The corner goes up in the air and brings the elbows down.

Now lie back on the floor and sit up. Put your legs crossed; lean on your left hand behind you. Now lean on your right hand behind you and notice the difference. Try it again. See what happens with the left side. Look. Your head and chest do not move with your hand. Try it on the other side—look—the whole body is turned, so that it is easy to do. Try again with both sides and notice the difference. Now lie on your back. Note how the right shoulder blade is lying, and the right arm, and what you feel in your head, and which leg, which hip joint lies better, which part of the chest contacts the floor better, and remembering what we did before, move your left leg to the left, and now slowly move the right leg to meet the left. Now move both legs gently, as if you were to lift your head as we did in the morning, and then move both legs a little to the right, and back to the left; but observe now how different the movement is to the right and to the left. Observe, what does the right side of the chest do, what does the right hip joint do, and then move to the right and back to the left. See whether your legs go a little bit more to the right than before. Those for whom it's difficult, do it in small little steps to the right, small little steps to the left. Only observe the difference of the movement in your chest, shoulders, arms, and neck, your spine, sternum, clavicles, and hip joints, and while you do that, any strain you feel is only in your head. To succeed in a short time, you must reduce your will power. If you can make the movement slowly, then you'll find that the strain goes.

It is the urgency to do something in a given time, that interferes with many, many actions, some of the most important actions. In love, making love, people are unwilling to give themselves the necessary time to do it; in fact it doesn't matter if you do it in another half hour, but when it comes out like something that has to be strangled, just now or not, the trouble starts. People do that in other parts of their lives, not only in their sexual life. In most of the things that are done wrongly, a person is actually straining to go beyond his ability and therefore he feels inferior and unable to cope with life, and goes to a psychiatrist. So let the time stretch a little longer, that means make your watch go a little slower and you'll see how life improves so fast that it is really a pity that the watch doesn't stop all together—for a few seconds at least. Now slowly get up, by turning to any side you like, walk around and feel each side of your face. Which side of the face is hard and what do you feel? Walk, check your legs, your hip joints, your chest; walk around yourself to the right, to the left; move and you'll see one side is so different from the other, that it is hard to believe. How is it that in a lifetime you never felt such differences in yourself? You see, they are genuine; you all are built like that. Now, what do you feel in the right side of the face—and to which side does your head turn easier?

You will see then that that side of yourself is prepared for movement. Now, organize yourself so that you are generous with yourself, at least as generous as I am with you. Now observe yourselves, look, examine, and then forget the whole damn thing. Forget it. Thank you. (Applause)

CRAWLING AND WALKING

Would you please stand. As you stand, put your right hand on the floor, in front of you somewhere. Some people put their hands on the floor and have the knees bent too much or too little. It doesn't matter, but some have the knees straight as if it were a rule that you have to touch the floor having the knees straight. Leave your knees bent, and in order to touch the floor with your hand move your pelvis right and left. You can't do this easily unless you do something with your knees. Observe whether your pelvis moves right and left the same amount; one knee bends and one straightens. But if you have them both straight, the movement is done elsewhere in a different way altogether. With your right hand on the floor move your pelvis a little bit to the right, a little bit to the left. Most people will leave their heads hanging. Note you all look down; no one looks upwards. Straighten slowly, and move about a pace or two. Do the same thing with your left hand. Now stop: get up and make another pace or two. Move about and again put both hands on the floor. Put your feet and knees together, and then move your pelvis a little bit to the right, a little bit to the left. When you touch your feet, touch the toes too. Now stop it. Again move about a pace or two. Go back, and touch the floor with both hands, move the left foot towards the right foot. Move slowly taking your pelvis a little bit right and left. Open your knees again. Put both hands one near the other on the floor. And now put the right foot near the left. Then go down and get up very slowly. When you bend don't straighten in one go. Take it a little bit at a time. Now, put both hands on the floor, and then take the right foot, backwards a bit, then forward, to the right, to the left. Lift your foot from the floor and put it back where it was, or at a place where you feel, "Ah, here, it's easier." Stand again, slowly and put both hands on the floor. Now move the left foot a little bit toward the front, then backwards, then to the right, to the left, and find the position of your foot where it is neither forward nor backward nor to the right, nor to the left, but where you feel you can carry weight on it and change. Do the same thing with your right hand, and again stand on all fours, and move the right hand forward and backwards a little bit and right and left, and find the position where it is neither forward nor backward nor right nor left but just neutral. Do the same thing with your left hand. You see, there are four points on the floor, which are characteristic of a person almost like a fingerprint. They remain practically the same through life until there are major changes in the body. Therefore, as soon as we get clear about it, you're able to do movements that you are not used to, and very fast ones too.

Would you please put your hands on the floor, and lift the right hand and the left foot and put them in the place where they would support you best, and easiest. Now do the same thing with the right foot and the left hand. While you do it, pay attention to your breathing and make no change. Maintain a shallow breath. Continue for yourself a few times, alternating along each diagonal. Now observe your neck. Do you stiffen your neck and immobilize your eyes? Now that's enough.

Stand up, walk a little bit, just enough to become less stiff. For most people stiffness is produced by the non-familiarity of the situation; we will make frequent breaks, so that you won't have pain. Now, slowly put your hands back again on the floor. Please lift your right hand and foot. Ah, you have to displace your left hand. So your hand was not in the right place. When a movement is properly done it must be such, that in the situation in which you are, you should be able to undertake any movement in any direction without a preliminary rearrangement.

Now, put your hands on the floor again, and find a way in which you can go diagonally and right and left. Lift your right hand and foot. You don't need to lift it a lot. And now your left leg, and hand. Observe that you return to a different position. Now try diagonally again. All your movements should start easily from the situation. Suppose you put your feet closer together than your hands, just a little bit. Try it. Your hands now will be wider. If you try the diagonal, it may be easier, it may not be. Now try lifting the right side and then the left. This movement is certainly easier, because the further you put your feet apart, the bigger your rotation to bring the weight to the other side; if your feet are too wide, it's very difficult to lift right and left. So try to make your feet as wide as possible; then put your hands down and then lift the right hand and the right foot (laughter). Can you see how difficult it is? Well, that's too wide. Make it a little—now look. Now you see something very funny. Once you get to understand the principle—you can do it wide and narrow and any way you wish. That is learning; you have a free choice. Take a break and walk a little bit as before.

Now go back to the floor again with your hands and feet neither too wide nor too narrow. But you have to learn something else now. Should your feet point in the same direction, parallel to each other? We don't know. Twist both your feet so that your heel is outward as much as possible. Now try to do one of the movements. (laughter) Put both heels inward and again try lifting the right hand and foot and try the diagonal. That is obvious, it makes life too difficult. Now, take them outward. More to the limit of what you can. And lift the right hand and the right foot, or lift the right foot diagonal. Between those two extremes find the most comfortable position. You see? That's better. Your feet can't be parallel. Only in walking are they parallel, not in standing. If they're parallel standing, then the standing is cockeyed. Now move about a little bit and, standing on your spot with your feet not touching nor parallel, put your feet parallel. Can you see? When your feet are parallel, all the other toes get crooked. Would you please put your hands on the floor and, hop, taking both feet off the floor. Put your feet closer to your hands and a little bit away until you find the most comfortable position. Continue hopping and watch, when you go forward, how much your feet open and you don't force them to be parallel.

You *can* do anything, you can also enucleate your eye, and cut your tongue. You see if someone tells a lie, you can cut out his tongue, so they never tell a lie afterwards. It was done in history; it's being done now in any of the advanced countries like Iran, Pakistan, Saudi Arabia. Now would you please put your hands on the floor. Now again put your hands too much forward, and take them backwards, near to your feet and find the position where you could lift both hands and lift both feet alternately. It should be as easy to lift your hands as your legs. Observe that the lifting of your legs should be the same speed, the same quality, and with the same amount of preparation. Otherwise you lose the purpose of what we are doing. Walk around a little bit, and take your place again. Put both hands on the floor and your feet, and observe the four points on the floor. Retain the configuration. Try slowly to walk around yourself to your right, so that your movement does not interfere with your breathing; it remains shallow. You'll see that your knees must point outwards and your feet point outwards. There is no other way to do it properly. Stand up, rest a little, make a few paces, and now walk to the left, round yourself. Observe, what do you move first? What next? And how do you do it? Slowly, gently.

Would you please stop, lie on the floor, rest a little bit and observe, where do you feel the change? Roll to the right and get up in one movement. Would you please put your hands on the floor and walk backwards. Observe how you do it. And then walk forward, and return to your position. Stand on your hands and knees on the floor. Now, crawl forward; how will you do it? You don't make the same movement as you did in the standing position. Can you see? It's very funny. Now walk backwards. Now watch, it's not the same as what you did on your feet; it's diagonal crawling. Now get on your feet and your hands and then observe what it feels like to go backwards. You do the two, the right side and the left side. It means there are two ways of walking.

Horses walk differently from kangaroos and other animals. The diagonal crawling is an advanced crawling. When children learn to crawl this way they are ready to stand. Now stand again on your hands and on your knees, and now crawl as you did. The hand and the leg of the same side must go together, otherwise it's not the same thing.

Have you ever thought that when a crocodile, who has a head and a neck 3 feet long, leaves the water, and walks, he has the world stable in front of him? Can you imagine, with his long head, if he did the side-to-side walking? His head would go right and left, and he wouldn't know where his food was or whether there was an enemy near. Therefore—it's a very funny thing, all living creatures maintain the head, eyes, ears, on the food, on the bait, on the danger while the body does anything that is necessary to attack or to escape. This is the basis of how the nervous system is organized. If we cannot organize ourselves in this way, we feel that we have a bad posture, and that our breathing is poor.

And it makes no difference how much we practice breathing exercises. Some spiritual teaching is in fact the kind of thing that we do, but it wasn't realized that you could teach a principle such as this to anyone. So people spend a lifetime to get the feeling that we get in one lesson. The nervous system grows as a result. Parts that didn't function, get into function, and then when this function is complete, another more delicate part has grown sufficiently and takes over the function and helps it. At the start the different parts of the brain make it easier to walk from right and left without separation, or differentiation between the hand and the leg. Until a certain age, a baby can't do the diagonal walking because the parts of the brain that make the diagonal possible have not developed.

Some people retain the undifferentiated walk for the rest of their lives. Now, watch, why do people, when they walk, move their hands? Get up, and walk, and see which hand goes with which leg. You'll find that you won't realize which goes with which. Can you see what happens? The pattern is the same as the diagonal cross crawling, just like the crocodile, so that the head can remain in the middle, but the tail will move to keep balance. With us our pelvis moves, so that the head can be directed the way you want it. Now watch, can you tell the movement is not quite exactly diagonal in standing? What moves first, your hand or leg? Now you'll see that if you move your hand and leg really together, you'll walk like the German army, and the Russian army imitates the German army with straight legs, bang, bang, bang, bang. It doesn't matter whether you're a communist or a fascist, you are the same idiot. (laughter)

Just to see the importance of the things we do learn, put your right hand on your right leg and go ahead and walk forward. When your hands and legs go together, what has to move? Can you see how much twisting you do with your pelvis? Put both hands on both thighs and walk. This walk is the same as the first primitive crawling. There are people who walk like that. Some will twist their shoulders instead of their arses. Now do it, move the shoulders instead of the pelvis. You also must move your head. Now go straight forward, and move only your pelvis, and keep your eyes on a speck on the window. Then you'll find out that you have to move both pelvis and shoulders. And that little movement of rocking the hands makes it possible to keep your head directed to the speck. The important thing is not that it is so. The important thing is that some people here have been in their body (that's the way a woman talked to me this morning) at least ten years, and they did not know that they were moving in that way. It's only when you know what you're doing that you can really do what you want. Would you walk simply, and see what you do with your arms now. It's diagonal. Now walk so that your right foot is forward, your left hand is back. Move your hands in a very big movement, and see immediately what you do with your legs; you begin to bang with your foot like one of the soldiers. You do that because you cannot twist your pelvis, and you

want to maintain your head in the position where you are free
to look wherever you want. Continue moving your hands up
to the horizontal, and you'll find that your pelvis doesn't have
to move. Some people think it looks nice. (laughter) It is no
good if you bend your knees. Then you are neither fascist nor
communist; it must be a straight leg, and the foot must bang.

Stand on your hands and on your feet. Note that just as
there are four points on which you lean, there are also four
lines: the line that joins the hands, the line that joins the feet,
and the two lines that join the hand and the foot. Now continue as you are but listen first: lift your right foot off the floor,
and bend your right leg at the knee so that you can turn your
pelvis to sit facing at right angles on the floor. Your knee
crosses the line between the left leg and the left hand. Now try
the movement starting from the position standing on your
hands and feet and you will bend your right leg, lift your foot
and then turn your knee to cross the line between your left
foot and hand, but at the same time you will sit on the floor
facing the left.

You know, it's so complex, because it is simple, but as we
don't know what we are doing, it's very difficult to say it in
words. Now try slowly and see what happens. Gently, learn for
yourself and keep quiet a moment. Now, if you can't see, look
at others, and you'll see that if you don't put the right thigh
completely on the floor with the knee, you're bound to let your
pelvis fall to the floor. The pelvis makes a continuous, simple,
curve. But your pelvis is the power station, and if it is haywire
how can you use it? Make it simple, easy, comfortable, so that
it takes no time to it. If you fall, you will hold your breath.
Slowly, now that is good enough.

Why don't you walk a few paces and see how your walking
is different? We did only a few movements; can you feel something different in the way the right leg walks, the left leg
walks and the pelvis? Lie on your back, and note which part,
which hip joint, which side of the pelvis is in better contact
with the floor. The places in yourself closer to the floor are

places where you have stopped doing useless work. Now, roll to the other side and stand there on your hands and on your feet and just think of doing the same thing with your left foot. Think through the movement, so that when you try it, it is as perfect as your thinking. You have already made all the mistakes on the other side, you know them, and if you know what you're doing, you should be able to do what you want on the left side. If you made a mistake, it will not be a disaster. We make mistakes, all our lives, anyway, with all the learning. So think it through, and then try it, and you will see that the side that you thought through straight away is easier and more comfortable than the side on which you learned the movement.

Now would you please stand on the hands and the feet as before, then think out the movement; once on the right and once on the left, and repeat. Then stand up gently, and see how you would enhance it, and connect it with another movement on the left, so that you make a smooth, continuous movement without falling in between, or jumping. Now watch what your pelvis does and how your head remains practically in the middle. If you do the movement very fast you'll see that your head will be absolutely in the middle later. Now there are very funny, minor little differences which make an enormous difference, and people don't realize it. Watch, keep on doing the movement and as you lift the foot off the floor, watch what the pelvis does; look up and down. Now don't lift your foot, and observe what happens. If you don't lift your foot, that minor thing makes that enormous difference. Find it out for yourself. If you don't lift your foot, your pelvis goes to sit God knows where; in fact, three feet away from one position to the other. Can you see how different muscles react altogether in a different manner in different situations? Yet some people cannot tell the difference. Now lift your foot and notice how the pelvis sits back practically in the same place in between the hands. Lie on your back and take a rest.

Where do you feel the breath starts? At the beginning when

the air comes in, which part moves first, and which goes into movement just gradually, afterwards, and you'll find that the part that starts first, when you breathe in, starts first also breathing out.

Alright, would you please stand on your hands and on your feet again, and now see, if you sit to the right—lifting your foot, your left hand is not needed. So do the movement to the right taking the knee through and lift your left hand and then go back to the other side and as you go past the middle lift your right hand. Observe, if you move the pelvis too far from one side to the other you won't be able to do the movement as we're doing now. Notice, your pelvis is now coming to stop exactly between your hands at the place which is just between your feet when they are standing. In fact, if you let down a plumb-line from your sex, that's where your anus sits. Making as little movement as necessary, change over your legs. Now you can make a little hop and change over your legs. Make one hop, and take your hand away.

Now those who are tired put your hands on the floor in your imagination. If you think it through carefully, you will advance more than by doing 50 movements. Do nothing, and think, then lift your left hand, and think that you put your hand back, lift your pelvis in one go and change over. [Moshe comments to someone in group.] No, that's not thought through, your thinking was broken by the halt of your breath; there was no complete thinking. The whole process must be thought through; it doesn't matter if it takes a minute to think of every detail; the next time you do it, it will take ten seconds and then the third, a tenth of a second, and then you'll be able to do it without being tired. Choose one of the correct positions for thinking, so that you will remind your intentional cortex of the whole pattern. And now, hop as fast as you can, but without hurry or confusion. Most of you are tense and in a hurry. Try to distinguish between going fast and going in a hurry. Just stand as you did at the beginning with all your hands on the floor. Note only what it feels like now to lift your right foot and right hand, and try diagonally lifting your right hand and left foot. Move both hands, and move both feet. Observe whether it's easier. Get up, walk around. Can you see we have made the impossible feasible, the difficult easy, and the easy comfortable to do.

Now, we can make a break, because we have done more than an hour's hard work. (applause)

LESSON FIVE:
THE RIBS AND ROLLING

Lie on your back. Spread your legs a little bit more than your shoulders, but not very much. Then join the fingers of your hands and place them on the chest, at the lower ribs where you're comfortable. Very slowly lift your right elbow, gently, so that the wrist of your right hand remains where it is. Your hands are at right angles with your body. Increase the movement a little bit; that means that your elbow lifts from the floor, and observe that you make such a minute movement.

Now what could you do to improve, to make the movement easier, lighter, and of course more extensive?

Observe; where is the difficulty? How do you interfere with lifting your elbow easily? Should your elbow be drawn away from your body when you lift it? Should it go away from the body or near the body? You can see that lying relaxed your arm is inclined about 35 degrees. The chest is higher. Therefore the elbow must first go away from the body, if you want to lift it, because it's in a shortened position.

Many of you do something with your shoulder and clavicles, and chest, which prevents lifting. If your elbow does not move away from the body, you lift with an effort which you don't realize. As you'll see, most of us are so wired that we lift and also lift the wrist, which is futile; it's not necessary. If you lift your wrist, you can't lift your elbow higher, or if you lift it higher, your right hand leaves your body. In other words: most shoulders don't move to their full ability.

Now you saw that yesterday, when you explored the surface around you. Your right arm changed as you moved because that allowed your shoulders and clavicles to move away from your chest. Now would you please stop and do it with the left elbow and feel the difference. Now with both elbows together. Now do it with both elbows and lift your head. Your head includes the skull, the face and the hair, so lift your entire head. Now your elbows will lift above your chest without the wrists lifting and the lower part of your chest flattens. This is important to your back, as the lumbar region is pressed to the floor.

Now you'll notice a funny thing. Do the movement with the help of your head again and see how wide your elbows spread and how high they are above the floor. Once you experience the movement with your head lifted, you can do the same movement without using your head. Try, and you'll see, you can lift the elbows the same amount. In fact it's not the head that makes the difference. It's what happens in your chest in flattening and what happens in lifting the shoulders. Your body and the ribs behind organize as if you lifted the head. The learning happens within 10 seconds. Now do it again with your head and find out that in fact you can do it without your head as well as with your head. Stop it, lower your arms and observe; what has happened to your shoulder blades, your breathing, the way your arms lie?

Rejoin your fingers as before, but with the nonhabitual interlacing of the hands. Some of you don't know what I mean. (Moshe demonstrates changing his hands so that first the right index finger is over the left and vice versa.) The right index over the left is one way, and the left over the right is another way; for one this is the habitual, for somebody else that's the habitual. Again lift your elbows with your hands interlaced the nonhabitual way. Now once you have them as wide as you can lift them, then lift your head, and notice the increase of the movement. Slowly move your right leg to join the left, and now slowly lift the right elbow, as if your right elbow will move with your body until it's pointing to the ceiling. Do it at first in your imagination and you'll find yourself beginning to move in actuality. Now think of rolling on the left side, and your whole body will roll to the left.

Don't succeed from the start, because if you succeed from the start you'll leave your spine and chest in the same rotten position. Now stop the movement, stay as you are and watch; instead of interlacing the fingers, put your right arm in the crotch of the left elbow. Your right hand lies underneath your left arm. Do the same movement as we did before, trying to roll to the left by lifting the right shoulder and elbow. Now if you roll to the right, you'll lean on the floor on your right arm, and the back of your left hand moves your elbow away. If you go slowly you find that it happens by itself, provided your nervous system realizes the necessity of doing that. Continue and observe how you roll to the left. Can you find out how to take your right elbow in the air in order to make the rolling gradual? Now go back; observe what happens to your chest. It now flattens as it did when your hands were on your lower ribs —and your back is rounder, not straighter. That is what makes it possible to roll. Now go back and observe that you get longer and your chest lies differently. When you roll, which part of your body begins to roll? Observe that to begin to roll, your lower ribs and chest and spine must have a peculiar organization to make an easy movement. And to continue the rolling should be as easy as to start. Observe what you do with your head at the end of the movement. Perhaps if you lifted your head and let your head come forward while you roll with your whole body together, the movement will be continuous.

Do you remember we talked about the tonus, the way the body contracts? When something is difficult, there's disorganization. Do you remember what we said about learning? That to increase your sensitivity you must improve your organization. And by organization we saw that the amount of contraction of the smaller muscles and the bigger muscles should be of the same degree. When the movement feels easy and light, then the entire body is contracting in the same way. As we said, we cannot measure work; we can only measure disorganization. Disorganization feels difficult, disagreeable.

Now change over the way you hold your hands so that they are reversed from the position we just used. Think of rolling to the right, but go gently. Your feet and body are not in the middle, and therefore if you go fast you won't learn anything. We are doing the movement that is symmetrical to what you did before. Obviously your legs must be moved with your body somehow. No, don't move them in one go. If you do that, you will do something that you understand. I want you to *feel,* so remember what you did when you rolled to the left. Make it possible for the body to do it now. Your legs can't remain on the left. If they remain on the left you've changed position. [To some members of the group] You're not rolling right and left, but you're rolling right and cockeyed.

Will you please lie again, correct your middle point in the direction you put your legs, cross your fingers, and put your crossed hands on your lower ribs. Now lift your right elbow and roll to the left, slowly, gently, and note only how you organize yourself to roll, and which part is the last to roll. Lie on your back again. Why should you roll with your knees held together like a cerebral palsy child, who can't take them apart? Are you protecting your innocence? (laughter) Observe what you do; do your hands participate in your rolling?

Roll on any side, and let your hand leave the body; you'll find only that your wrist must let go. Now, lift your right elbow and roll to the left, and then you'll see you can't do it unless your left elbow goes away from your body. Stay rolled to the left; where did your hands have to go? To roll this way, they must turn palms outwards, and move away from your body. Find out at which point of your rotation they must turn to make the rolling easy. Now think, while you're rolling to the left, that you could straighten your right elbow. Straighten it a little bit. Then you'll find that it gets easier to roll. Change the interlacing of your fingers, and do the same thing to the other side. You can't straighten your elbow without your hands going away from your body, with the palms out. Go from one side to the other.

Stop it, now again put your right hand in the crotch of your elbow, and your left hand underneath. Roll to the left and stay there. Move your upper elbow away from your body. Now draw in your stomach, and push it out. Flatten your chest. As you draw in the stomach, you'll see that your hands and your elbows go away from your body. At the same time something happens in your spine which is very helpful. Draw in your stomach, while you move your elbow, and if the elbows don't move, your stomach is not really drawn in. Bend your knees a little more. Otherwise, your concern with your balance interferes with the movement. As you draw in your stomach notice that you have to move your breast, and your chest must deform in an unusual way. And if you watch carefully, you will see that you want to bend where you normally don't. I mean for you to round the spine which helps the shoulders go forward. The inability to do this movement explains why it was so difficult to lift both shoulders at the beginning. Now change over your hands, and roll over to the other side slowly. Continue the same movement on this side. Of course now, your left elbow goes away from your body and as you draw your stomach in, your lower ribs flatten. This changes the curve in your back in a way that only clever athletes, acrobats and babies, can. That is, before they are taught by teachers and parents to behave correctly. Watch a baby at the age of two or three, who is not already deformed, walk. It's a pleasure to see how they move, like small kittens. Now notice, when you draw your stomach in, your head and shoulders must move towards your lower body and as you do this, your pelvis tilts so that your spine moves backwards. You draw together, as if your head were to join your knees.

Now slowly straighten yourself and roll on your back; join your fingers, and place your hands on your lower ribs. Lift both elbows and your head and see how they move now. Compare how well you lift with the movement at the beginning. That shows that you moved your shoulders, clavicles, and shoulder blades as they should have been able to move all your life before. Let that go and sit up, anyway you like. Cross your legs.

Now join your hands, interlace the fingers and place them just by the navel. Lower your head forward, and bring both elbows forward. How far forward can you bring them if you

lower your head? Now take your right elbow forward in between your legs. Then do the left. Organize your legs so that
you can touch the floor with one elbow and the other elbow.
Those who cannot, do it in your imagination. Do the same,
taking both elbows forward. Can you touch the floor with both
elbows? Now would you please stretch both legs more or less,
and put both feet standing. Interlace your fingers, place your
hands at your navel, and place both your elbows in between
your legs. Your legs will be as far apart at your knees as
possible so that your elbows will fit in between. But if it is
difficult, start with one elbow and then slowly follow, placing
your other elbow between your knees. You will find that after
another three movements, both elbows can be placed in between your knees. And now very slowly and gently squeeze
your elbows with your knees, and organize the rest of the body
to help. You'll find that you have to round your back, the
lumbar spine, and your head lowers. A normal person should
be able to join the elbows like that in front. But for most it is
very difficult. You see, we are very far from using the thorax
properly. It is the thorax which connects the source of power,
our pelvis, with our head, the source of orientation and intentional movement. The link doesn't work, and the reason is
that we never did actually try to do what we wanted. We
always did what somebody found right for us to do. For myself
this was true from my childhood through the university, and
therefore the link, the ability of doing what *I* wanted was
eliminated by making the link between the power and the
intention unavailable. Ida Rolf understood this. For she made
her first lesson, not on the head, nor on the pelvis, but here at
the link, and if you ask her why she did it, she felt she had been
trying to find the most effective way to start.

Change over your hands and interlace your fingers the non-
habitual way, and again put one elbow and then the other
between your knees. You will be astonished that once you do
half a dozen movements, you will find that you can touch the
floor. Slowly. Get there with the greatest ease. And now put
both hands inside and you find that it's easy. Some people will

find that with open legs like that they can touch the floor with both elbows. Then you'll find dozens of people in a group who can do it almost from the start.

There's a bearded man there who does the exact wrong thing. He does what he has learned. You think that if you stretch your back until it aches for a week, then you've done a good thing. But you're hurting and you'll have back pain tomorrow. So think, and find out how you can organize yourself to do it. That's better. As you continue on the left, try to lift your left leg a little. Make two movements like this with the left twice and with the right twice. Then you'll find that you can touch the floor. But if you force yourself you will only ruin your back, and you won't touch.

Now think of lifting the right leg, while you take your right elbow downwards. And now while you take your right elbow down think of lifting your left leg. Lift it twice and you'll see that the right elbow will touch the floor. Do it the other way with your left elbow and right leg several times, gently. Now rock your body like that, right and left, and touch with one elbow or the other. Put both elbows in between your knees, and see how far you can go down, and see how much you can squeeze your elbows between your knees. It's incredible that fat women, old women do it here, now. Is that a compliment or an insult to be a fat old woman? What do you think? It's an insult by the standards of very self-minded people. You cannot be very different from what you are; the more you like yourself the better will be your life.

Now stop that, cross your arms, bend and roll until you can half lie on your pelvis without lying on your back. Roll inwards with your legs slowly, but don't roll to lie. The difference between lying and sitting is much less than you think. Find a way to a minimum, which makes the difference between lying and sitting. Switch and sit; now lie. You can see that unless your entire self is there from the toes to the head, you can't sit and lie as you wish. Try again. No, that's folly; you hold your breath; it should not be held. You are not bending the upper part of the body. Make very tiny little movements, so that you can sit and lie at will, and make the minimum change. When you lie, the back of the pelvis and the small of the back touch the floor. Put your head on the floor, and stop. Now you are lying. Now reorganize yourself as you are, to the same position as you were, and sit. The way your pelvis touches the floor makes the difference between sitting and lying. One way if you stop doing, you are sitting, and the other way if you stop doing, you're lying. Your knees need to be open. Those who sit easily will have their knees outwards, going apart. The legs are like two tentacles going to make the balance with your head and shoulders. [Moshe answers a question.] Most people can't round their backs properly to do this movement. So we did that first to make the movement possible. If we start with what we do now nobody would succeed.

The movement should be reversible. You should be able to stop at any point. If you let your entire body be present in your mind from your toes to your head, then the movement will be absolutely easy. Now put your hands forward and your feet forward and now try again. As you get up you can also lengthen your arms and knees. Then everything bends together to go back.

Now that's enough.

Would you please get up slowly. Put both hands on the floor and stand on all fours as you did before. Observe how easily your hands come on the floor, and how much you bend. Look at this gentleman there, the oldest of the lot. He does it as well as anybody else. Look how his knees are apart, how his feet are. When you started in the morning, can you recall how he did it with both feet near each other? [To the gentleman.] Do it as you did in the morning when you couldn't do it. That's too well done. (laughter) Now you're bending your knees, and you couldn't this morning. In any case the improvement is better than any one of you because he started with bad knees and feet and now he does it as well as anybody else. Can you see it has nothing to do with age—it has to do with ability to learn. That means the quality of the brain, that is all.

Thank you very much (applause)

LESSON SIX, PART I:
ARM CIRCLES

Will you please lie on your right side; let your right arm lie
with the back of the hand on the floor. Now please move it as
it is. Move it around wherever you wish, where you can feel
and explore the floor; first move it in an arc, towards the head,
and towards the legs. Now nearer to yourself, but start with
the back of your hand. You can also use the palm. But wherever you go you'll find there are places where you can only
move with the back of your hand. Your elbow can be straight,
or bent. Find it for yourself. You must have either your palm
or back of your right hand on the floor, not the tips of your
fingers.

Now, obviously you can't go any farther than your head will
let you. Your left hand can be placed wherever it's needed. It
is possible to go everywhere. But you can not do it just with
the palm, or with the back of the hand; there are absolutely
precise points relative to your spine where your hand must
turn. If you don't turn your hand, you won't be able to explore
all the space even if you kill yourself.

Go higher now and continue underneath your head. You
must lift your head a little and bring your arm below your
head, and place your head back on the floor. It is a movement
of your entire self. So think how other parts of yourself cooperate. Why do you have to hold the other arm in your pocket or
on your ass? Why can't you stretch the arm above your head?
If you don't need your other arm, then why do you need your
head? There's nothing you can do without your entire self
being mobilized. And your right arm doesn't have to be

straight at every moment. But you should be able to reach to its limit. Can't you reach behind you? No? You see? The limitation is in your brain, not in your body. And why can't you bend your knees? If you have to keep balancing, can you still explore the floor?

Would you please put your right hand in front of you with the back of the hand touching the floor? Bring your elbow near to yourself. Can you push your elbow underneath yourself? Ah, you could? If you use your left hand and your whole self, you will see it's possible. Put your left hand on the floor, and make it easy, and comfortable. Now, organize yourself so that it's easy to bring your right elbow underneath you. Help with your head, pelvis, and legs. Now continue to bring it back, and put it through like that, and then you'll learn that your left hand swings from behind your body to the front on the floor as your right elbow goes under yourself. Now when you return you must introduce the tips of the fingers of your right hand first. Continue until it's easy, and comfortable, and think: why did it not occur to you that you could explore the floor behind you? Do you hold your breath? Do you breathe hard? If so, obviously you are not doing the best you can. If not, when will you? Later it must be better than now. Use your hands to make it easy. Afterwards, if you want to do it without the help of your left hand, the movement will be the same. Now slide that hand underneath you in such a way that you can stop at any moment, and take it out without having to stop breathing, or breathing differently. Then you'll notice that the middle of your body, chest, and the middle of your spine does exactly what we learned to do this morning. So draw your stomach in to help.

Now if you can take your right hand under your head and under your right buttock, you can make a complete circle if you let your hand turn at the precise points relative to your body.

Make this complete circle without stopping, in a light continuous movement with no pressure change on the floor. Can you organize yourself in such a way that your hand can slide around with the same pressure whether it is with its back on the floor or the palm? But don't take your hand underneath your pelvis; leave it on the floor.

Now reverse direction and pay attention again to the parts of yourself that must cooperate. Your head lifts only at the precise moment you take your arm underneath. Your breathing is easy and the movement as uniform as you can make it. If you stiffen your legs, you hold your breath without knowing it.

Stop, lie on your back, put both hands on either side of the body, and observe what your right arm feels like, your left arm, the right shoulder blade and the left; notice how different they are. Now roll on the left to get up. Observe; which arm feels longer? How is your right shoulder different from your left? Now spread your feet a little bit. Which side is more forward? Make a fist with your right hand and take it forward and up, keeping your fist and arm in the same plane. Watch your hand as you lift it, and increase the velocity, taking your arm in a circle. Keep your knees soft, pelvis soft; let your head and eyes follow your fist, and go faster. Now you'll see that when you go really fast your head will remain stationary. Now change the direction, and think how would you do it faster, without hurry. And you'll see that you can't make it faster unless you involve your hips, and your legs, and your ankles, and your toes, and your breath, and everything you have. That's right. Now stop it. Now walk around and compare the sensation in your right hand and left, in the right side of the body and the left side, the right leg, and the left. (laughter and talking)

LESSON SIX, PART II:
MAKING A CIRCLE WITH YOUR HIP

Lie on your right side. Have your knees bent normally. Please stay as you are. Now lift your left knee and draw it nearer to yourself, and then move it away from the floor. Make a small circle with your left knee. Lift it near yourself, and away towards the ceiling, and increase the radius of the circle. But observe that some of you stop making the circle as soon as you come a little bit over your body. It's impossible to make the circle, if you take your knee just over your body. You end up making a straight line downwards. If you want a circle, you must find resources in your self to continue the circle. There is only one way to do it.

It's very funny, you are not finding it. Do anything you like, but make the biggest circle possible with your left knee and mobilize everything you have to do so. Don't change the direction, go in the same direction but complete the circle. By the way, there's no question of doing it with your foot; the knee is the highest point. This is similar to what we did before with the elbow and then afterwards with the whole arm. If you don't reach the floor with your left thigh on the other side, you will not have a circle. In other words, you still have to involve the rest of yourself. Your thigh must turn to the other side, and to the floor. But don't put your foot standing on the floor. It is incredible that people have so few resources in themselves. . . . What did you do with yourselves all the years? Didn't you know that you have legs or a head, or arms?—it's time.

Now would you make that circle uniform? You can reach every point, but not if your spine is stiff. Go slow. You'll find that you have to turn, and move your spine between your shoulder blades and chest. For some that part is so stiff and unworkable that you no longer have an idea that you need it.

Now stop for a minute. *Think* how you do it. Would you please lift your knee from the position where it is now, and turn your knees to your left until the left side of your thigh and leg lie on the floor? Your whole self must organize itself in a way which is not familiar. Now begin to make a circle with that knee but in the opposite direction. Now can you see that you can not make a complete circle unless you touch the floor. You could make a bigger circle only if your pelvis was lying on a high pillow. Then your knee could move more. Continue the movement and observe which parts of yourself do not allow you to make the movement properly.

Stretch out both legs straight. Feel the difference between one hip joint and the other. And now note, what is the line of stress which joins your left hip joint with your right shoulder blade? Can you feel on the floor that this line is different from the line joining the right hip joint to the left shoulder blade? Now would you please roll on the opposite side from which you rolled last time, and get up; walk around and feel what it feels like with a hip joint that has been doing what a hip joint should be able to do; note the difference between the left leg and the right leg, the left hip joint and the right hip joint. Stop somewhere, and begin to move your right fist as you did before; make a few circles in one direction, and the other, and just note how it now is. What does the left hip joint do for your movement? What does the left leg do? Is the movement easier? Is the circle quite different from before? Note the grace of the movement; look at the continuity of the movement; how is that? Watch what the left knee and the left hip joints do in order to make this possible. Now increase the speed, and notice, is that the same speed as before, or a bit faster? Ha, look at that; the average speed of all the people has increased markedly. Change the direction. Can you keep your breathing

shallow? Stop it, walk around and observe how much movement there is in one leg and the other. Which leg makes the
bigger pace? Observe, it is not necessarily the leg that we
worked with, because the improvement on that side allows the
other leg to do better. Your right hip joint may not allow the
left one to move and vice versa. So it's not enough to think; you
can mislead yourself. The question is—observe what you're
doing really. Now walk backward and see what happens now;
which leg makes the good step? Walk forward.

Now stand and do the following. Move your right leg to the
right; lift it and take a bigger step to the right. Then bring the
left leg towards the right, and spread your legs apart using
your left leg. Make it larger, and go over with the right. Continue and then make the largest steps that you can both ways.
Is there a difference between one leg and the other? Now make
a step and join both feet together; make the biggest step sideways with the left leg, and immediately, go to the right and
make the largest step, and join them. Then the largest step to
the left, and join them. Now observe, which leg leads you
better? Which leg feels less stiff, feels cleverer to do what you
want it to do, and moves thereby from the hip joint?

Will you please lie on the floor, on the left side, and now
think, without actually moving; how would you explore the
floor with your left hand taking your arm around in a large
circle as you did before? Imagine where you will turn your
hand and how your hand will pass under your head and under
your body. Make it so that your imagination is closer to what
you actually feel, and then change the direction in your mind.
Test it out and discover whether you have improved further.
And now would you please make three complete circles with
your knee. And as you continue feel what happens in your
spine in between the shoulder blades, and the upper and lower
part of your chest. Usually you don't move this way. Now
make three circles in the other direction. Then make one
circle with your right leg, and one circle with the left in such
a way that you continuously switch from one to the other.

Continue so that you make two circles with the right leg,

and then two complete circles with the left. Which direction feels better to you? Reverse direction and start by taking your knee away from yourself. Immediately there are changes in the spine. If you go fast it won't be a circle. Now make two movements but let your feet go upwards and your knees straighten. Move your foot to make the circle. Make one complete circle with your right foot, and one more in the same direction, and change the direction of that leg. Slowly as you continue with your right leg, let your left leg come up, and alternate one leg and the other.

If you can do it now, at a later time you will find you no longer have a problem. A problem can be solved only with your intellect. But if you have a problem of movement, well the body will arrive there after you have the ability to organize differently. Later you don't need a new exercise, but you bring your body that you have now and its history to that moment and you should be able to cope better than before we did the lesson. In other words you organize your brain and body in such a way that you are capable of doing, and know what you are doing. You are then rigged out to fit the problem. Life is not made of problems that you solve with an exercise. What we are doing here is organizing ourselves. We can make that organization good now, so that if you had to face a problem suddenly, you would be able to negotiate it. For instance you should be able to reach with your hand faster and better in any direction than you did before. And also your hips and shoulders should help you to move better so that you don't have to prepare another exercise to solve a future problem.

DISCUSSION: THE EYES EFFECT THE MUSCULATURE OF THE NECK

[Moshe takes a question from a group member but interrupts.] Now what's your question? "In most people I see. . . ." Would you please stop? I have already severe criticism of your way of asking the question, but that doesn't mean I am trying to punish you and won't hear your question. I ask, what is *your* question? Instead of asking, "People with eyes . . . ?", think, wait, make it clear and make it your business to say: "My eyes don't serve me like that . . . that's my question." And I will explain. If someone comes to me for help, I ask him that simple question: what bothers you at this moment? And then some people will tell me: "Oh, I don't remember if it was on Thursday or Friday. I think it was Thursday afternoon in 1977 I went with my wife to Switzerland to ski, where I—surely it must have been late in the winter." Well, what bothers you now?" So he says "Wait a minute. . . ." And he wants to tell you the story the same way. I know that with this person I will have to work quite a time before I get to the thing that bothers him. So when that happens I say, "Thank you, I know already, will you please stand up and let me touch you." I touch, find out where the trouble is and do the lesson. Afterwards, when I have finished with that part which troubles him most, he says, "Yes, that happened years ago." I say, "I know, thank you, that's all."

Now what is *your* question? You'll find that with many people, their minds get blank and they cannot ask the question. So take your time. I did not intend to be personal, but asked the question in order to show you the way, and to elucidate the difference between Functional Integration, and other systems.

[The person asks the question again.]

Your eyes don't see better when your head is in one position or another, provided your head and eyes are well organized. In so far as the acuity of seeing is concerned, it does not depend on the movement of your head. If you look to your right as far right as you can, you'll find it very difficult to read small print. But in the normal range of movement of your eyes and head there's no connection between acuity of the seeing at the moment and the position of your head. Obviously it's not this that you asked. That you understand yourself. But in the course of a person's life, the head and eyes are absolutely so linked that I can with closed eyes take the back of your neck with my fingers and tell you whether you wear glasses or not, and if so how strong your right eye is and how strong the left. That is one of the questions which is at the foundation of the work. We have been dealing with it already in the last few days by thinking about the head and the pelvis. You use your head to explore and find the things you want to do outside of yourself, but the pelvis carries your head and provides the power to do it. So we talked about it. But to answer the question really properly I need an hour at least. Then you would have a better understanding of eyesight, something the whole world doesn't understand. Poincaré, the famous mathematician, wrote a book, *Science and Hypothesis,* and in that book he gives the foundation of Functional Integration. Had I read it before, I wouldn't have dared to do the work I've done. I would have thought that everybody knew it. It turns out he wrote in 1887 and made as clear an exposition of Functional Integration as I have been capable of doing. He talks about eyesight and why the world as it is seems stationary, and how this is the basis of geometry. Everyone accepts and knows that a triangle here will be a triangle in any place on earth, and will have the same properties; but they don't know that this has to do with our eyesight and the way our eyes function with our brain.

Do you know how the eyes are focused at birth and at death? Do they look out towards infinity or are they focused to see the nose? And what do we mean by focused? There are two ways of focusing. First there is the movement of the eyes going together and apart to see something close or far away. If you want to read, you have to bring the eyes closer, and they converge. Second, the muscles of the crystaline control the thickness of the crystaline, and therefore its refractive power. In old age the crystaline gets harder, the focusing doesn't work and many need glasses. Now that happens also to children. Most people find that they need glasses when they first go to school. If something were done to relieve the anxiety and emotional upheaval of children, they wouldn't need glasses at all. But no one pays attention to that. So people are fitted with glasses and they continue to wear them for the rest of their lives.

Now I'm telling you that this question has no answer. If you go to a good book on physiology, you'll find that different researchers, Helmholz, Young, Shaffer, and others, have a different answer. Each has done experiments to find out how it is. But only if you know how they did the experiments can you find out which is correct. With the kind of learning and training in our culture, our eyes and head move together, in one piece along with our hands, and arms. In the lesson that we did, why did I ask you to look at your fist, and how was it that you were able to turn your hand then?

Now look: if I don't watch my fist with my eyes, and my fist is outside my sight, I can't go any further, my shoulder is fixed. Because my eyes are fixed, my head cannot move; therefore my arm cannot move. When I look, I can go on, and make a complete circle. So you see the question asked is actually present in my mind. When I dictate and represent to you what you do, you succeed because I bypass those fixations and improper organizations of the self for the movement.

Now if you take your arm in a circle in the standing position, your arm must stay in the same plane, if you wish to go fast. Otherwise you will endanger the shoulder joint. That means the joint socket must be brought to the position to allow your hand to move and that cannot be done without your eyes following the movement. This has to do with the link between eyes and head that we learn in our culture in early childhood. Therefore you find that most people find it difficult to look one way and turn their head the other way. We will do that in a later lesson. Now let's see how the head is involved. To see clearly, you must move your head. Look, if my body and head are not organized to carry my head freely, and the connection between my head and pelvis is not properly organized—then, if I turn my head so far I cannot go on any further. That's the limitation of my sight. To go any further, either I break my neck vertebrae, *or* I bring the basis of the cervical spine in such a position that the relative movement of my head is sufficient to take me to the point where I need to go. If I turn my head to the right, the left sternocleido-mastoid muscle contracts, the other side is soft. The other muscles of the right side of my neck stiffen. If my habit of looking is that my eyes turn one way and I cannot turn my head the other way, the turning is restricted. But furthermore if I habitually turn one way in preference to the other, I will turn one direction with my entire body and the other with my head first.

Now I can tell by putting my hands behind someone's neck that these muscles are stiff and strained like springs, the others are soft and good muscles. Therefore I know now the person habitually turns to look and therefore I can bet one against a million that his left eye is the dominant eye. With that eye he sees, and so he turns his head that way. So this part of the movement of the whole horizon is soft and good, and the other one not, because that eye moves as the left hand in writing for a right-handed person. [Moshe directs his remarks to a woman in the group.] Now for you the left eye is the dominant eye. If I touch your head, you'll see that the two muscles that turn your head are very different. With your dominant left eye the left sternocleidomastoid muscle is easier and nimbler. The right is stronger but not better. The right does idiotic work and is stiff. The left is a real muscle, a good one.

All of you find the middle of your nose; now turn your head right and left. Can you see? She turns left at least twenty degrees more than to the right—without knowing it—because that is how she always moved. But this is so with your spectacles. Now take off your glasses and do the same movement. She turns more to the right, and less to the left. Do you know why? With her glasses she can see clearly only with the central part. To the outside the rims of her glasses interfere. She must turn her head more to bring her sight in the middle to focus. For a person who works with glasses, the glasses have already distorted the relationship between the eye movements and the head. These are biologically, anatomically, and functionally so linked together, that they are of primary importance for the organization of your movement.

Anyone who wishes to read a description can find it summed up in *Body and Mature Behavior*. But the original paper is by Magnus from Utrecht, who is a famous physiologist. In 1925 he published a very long article, reporting his discoveries on the normal eye reflexes and neck reflexes and the righting reflexes connected to the eye and then the righting reflexes of the neck, and then the combination, how the eyes influence the movement of the head, and how the neck reflexes are not independent of the eye reflexes, and the other way round. It's a very complex thing. If you look at modern books of physiology, they have at least 30–40 pages on that business of the eyes and the neck and standing. And that is a short introduction to answer your question.

Let us make it a little bit more concrete—talk itself means nothing. If you try it yourself, you'll see a funny thing. Look, if I turn my eyes to the left towards you and now I wish to stand up, my pelvis organizes itself so that one leg becomes rigid and strong to carry my weight and the other leg and side become limp and easily capable of turning. And if I sit back and am still turned, the leg on the side to which I am turned is stiff and the other, limp. Now, I hear a noise on the right and I turn to look right; my body is ready to move, to take off the twist from my neck and eyes and the right side is prepared. All the necessary strength in the muscles and the organization for action is established by the movement of my head *or* my eyes, or both. This is one of the essential mechanisms in life that you have organized from the time you were born. If you have worn spectacles or lenses, then there is a disorganization.

In my own case my eyes were improved in the last year with an implant in one eye and a lens in the other and my eyes focus a little better. Though I am now older, my movement and gait are easier and simpler than a year ago. Well, you wouldn't think that I am as clumsy as I am. (laughter) And that is actually what I explained to you, that in order for your legs to be free, your head and eyes must find themselves in the middle. Now, can you see, there are some questions that look very simple, but to answer them you'd find that you have to reorganize your entire life.

Now when I teach and introduce myself to a public that is unfamiliar with my work, I begin by having them turn and look in the same direction. That is easy and better organized than other movements. But there is a point where you cannot go any further without rearranging yourself. Then I show people an extraordinary thing, which they do not know. Most people believe that in order to go further you have to be supple, and have strong muscles, and be young. If they have rheumatism or torticollis they stop, and can't move any further. The whole movement is stiff, and the vertebrae can't move. For some there is pressure at one point in the spine and with the loss of movement that point gets arthritic, the cartilage is destroyed. Movement then is painful and a person is afraid he will break something if he continues. So I have them do something different. I tell them, do not do anything. Just keep your nose fixed in front of you and move your eyes to the other side, and come back, and repeat. Now I say, go back, close your eyes, and do the movement as you did before, just to the moment where you feel that you have reached the limit as before, that here you must change your effort. And it has changed about 10–15°. Now I say, keep your eyes fixed in front of you and take your head to the other side. Just three or four movements are necessary. Close your eyes, just organize yourself to do that movement which you felt right and stop where you felt that there's a change of effort. Again people increase. And I keep on showing them that they do movements which are contrary to everybody's experience, moving the eyes in the opposite direction where you want to get supple; no exercises, we just move in the opposite direction. And it does not matter how stiff they were before, whether or not they had rheumatoid arthritis, whether they were fat or not, whether old or not. People sometimes have an improvement of four to five times the amount they could turn before.

[Moshe speaks to the person who asked the question about eyes.] Try to do it now. Sit; look at me with your glasses so that you see me clearly. Now just move both your shoulders; can you see? Your habit is to move your head and eyes; now move your shoulders, and look at my nose. Not your hands, you see? That's the disorganization that your glasses have made for you. You'll get to improve it now. [The woman comments] "My sight has changed since I have been doing Awareness through Movement". Yes, of course it's better. But I want to show you and the group the importance of your question and the answer. Watch me. If I look at you, I turn the shoulder girdle, and I hold my hands there on my penis; can't you? Of course you can't, you haven't got a penis. (laughter) You can hold your hand on what you can and move the shoulders, and look at me. Do six movements, so that it becomes a familiar simple movement. You don't have to strain to do it well; breathe freely, shallow. Now stop. Gently, look to your right as far as it's easy, where you don't have to make an effort, turn your head and eyes to the right. [To the group] Watch how much more she turns that she did before. Turn to the other side. Look, an enormous improvement. How is it possible? And that's the answer to her question; that's Magnus' work, as I have uniquely applied it with Functional Integration.

A professor of physiology at the University of Chicago came to my place in Israel and did the lesson I just described. I did not know whether she was pleased or not, but she sat as if something very strange happened. At the end she told me, "I sit there and I am moved by this lesson." I say, "Why? What's in it?" She said. "For 25 years I have been teaching my students about eye reflexes, neck reflexes, tonic eye reflexes, tonic neck reflexes, the righting reflexes, and the combination. I taught Magnus' work. But it has never occurred to me to make it useful. (laughter) And so I thought, how silly my teaching is. I could have used this to improve the life of all my students, but I didn't—I only examined them to see if they understood what I taught."

MOSHE
AT
MANN RANCH

"Movement is Life; Without Movement,
Life is Unthinkable." — Moshe Feldenkrais

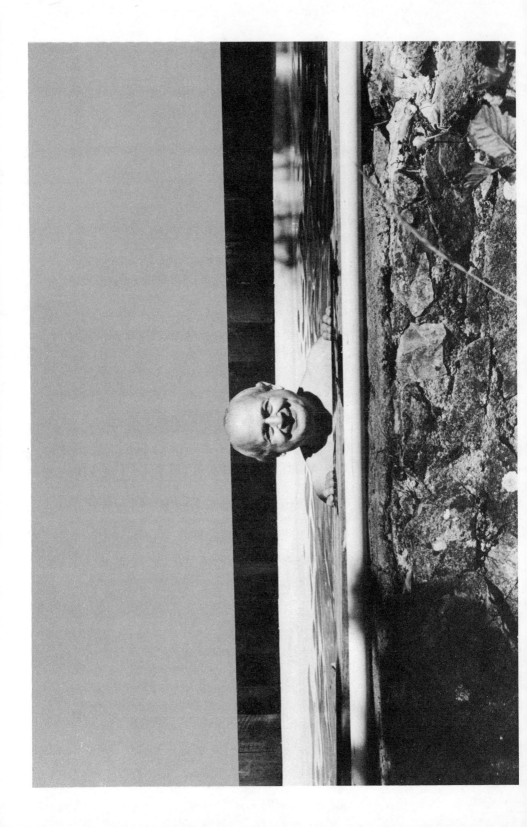

LESSON SEVEN:
THE MOVEMENT OF THE EYES ORGANIZES THE MOVEMENT OF THE BODY

Alright now, let us see how it works. Many of you have done this lesson before, but you'll find that when we do it now, that you will improve beyond any expectation, as you have already learned to be more supple from our previous lessons. Sit with your right leg back and left in front. You can see that intelligent people would support themselves with their left hand, even if it were not necessary. Here is someone in the group who has trouble with his hip joint and needs support. Well, any clever, intelligent surgeon would say, "It's an old hip; if you would like to move the thing, put in an artificial hip joint." But his hip joint is better than an artificial joint, provided he uses his brain as well as he can.

Now let's see whether what I say is just bunk, junk, or it works. So, lean on your left hand. Why? We could talk a whole hour on that movement alone. Now keep your hand like that, and please don't do anything with your body, just take your hand away. Can you see? As you take your hand away, you hold your breath and hold your body so that you won't fall. Now, obviously you have to keep the body balanced, and one side of the body has to work hard. Those muscles will be engaged in holding your body, and therefore you can kill yourself trying to make them supple. When a muscle is engaged in doing something, it can't do something else. In other words, you can't smoke a cigarette and kiss your beloved, because the mouth is busy sucking. Now don't lean on your hand and at the same time relax your trunk. Make any effort you like, the muscle can not relax. It is engaged because it is your intention to sit like that. Your motor or intentional cortex is organizing the performance of your intention. It can not be involved elsewhere. There is only one thing to do. Support the muscle so that it need not work.

So proceed to support yourself with your left hand. Can you feel the muscle is relaxed? Now I can train it. Let me repeat, if you want to relax the muscle, you don't have to ask it to relax; just support that member in such a way that that muscle becomes useless, and you will find that the human brain is so clever that as soon as it feels it's safe to let that muscle rest, it does it immediately.

That is how I work with people who, say, have a broken arm and cannot relax the shoulder. I bring a chair and support the arm in such a way that the nervous system eventually realizes that the arm is absolutely safe. Then the arm will have to relax, the shoulder will begin to move, and then I can with my hands give even greater security. When I attempt to move the shoulder, I will move the inside of the joint; I move the body around that joint. When it's finished, I say, "Take away the chair" and the person will say, "Ho, how is it, it's two years since I lowered it." Yet I never touched the arm at all.

Because you see what happens in the brain of the person: he's concerned with the intentional movement only, he intends to lift his hand. Now something went wrong, and he can't do it anymore; therefore he loses the entire ability to direct his arm.

What I do for him is this. Instead of moving the muscles in the way his brain is used to, I do the reverse. A muscle pulls from both sides equally at the insertion, and the origin, and doesn't know how to pull one side and not the other. Now the only thing is that when the heavy part lies there motionless, the other end of the muscle, at the hand for instance, does the biggest movement. Now, how do you do it? By finding a funny sort of thing: that your nervous system maintains your body stationary, and that you do this with such innocence since it's done from the first moment you are born. You must, otherwise you can't move a limb. It becomes like air, which you don't notice, you simply breathe. Now, when I get somebody who can't move, I don't start training his brain and tell them: look, you're going to do this movement. If he does it with the present image of his body, it will be a job as in physiotherapy. If you watch me, I keep that arm still, and move the body around that joint, so that the muscles are moved from the part where they usually are stationary. This is the reverse pattern of what is normal. Even for a normal arm the ability is limited. You saw it yesterday, and you improved your ability. When you turned your arm lying on the floor, you had to move your trunk and leave your arm under you on the floor. So you moved from the other end, which your brain had no experience of at all. That way you differentiated the pattern in the motor cortex so that it was suddenly capable of doing actions from either side. Do you remember the woman you saw me work with yesterday? She could not lift her arm. But I did not attempt to lift it, because she would immediately sense the limit of her movement and resist. That's what psychiatrists find, that a person is resisting. What do you do? You try to break the resistance. Or break the arm or make pain. Therefore as you come to the resistance point in psychiatry you get everybody crying and feeling miserable, and that's it. That's trying to break through your resistance. Now you see, when I find resistance, I don't break through the resistance. I support the arm in a stationary position where the person feels safe. You saw it on the videotape, but you did not pay any attention. And now with the arm supported and safe I can move the body to the point of resistance and it's gone. No resistance, no one knows even where it was. I moved the other side of the joint, which hasn't got the idea whether it's resisting or not resisting. Therefore I get the full movement of the arm in a few seconds, so that people look at it ten times and they don't see it.

Now here is another case. This woman couldn't move her head herself because she had an operation on her chest. I want to have her understand that there is a muscle that she cannot use. By supporting the shoulder I make the muscle useless by taking over its work and look, the muscle has nothing to do anymore. The pectoral muscle has nothing to do, and therefore, as her brain is a normal brain it will take her a few seconds to realize that there's no point in holding it. So she changes what she does. Now where was the point of resistance? No, I don't ask. I know where it was. Look to the front, and to the side, and to the back; there it is. Now once I do that, I can let go and the brain is clever enough to know with one experience that it is possible. As for the gentleman who needs support for his hip, I will manage to have his hip joint as nimble and as soft as anybody here, the youngest or the best, except of course if the joint is already so destroyed that it's beyond repair. But even in that case the movement can be restored. It may be painful afterwards. But I believe—he looks healthy enough, and it is only that common inability to think that stops him from improving. He knows that he is 74 and if he is 74 he must be able to move his hips as everybody else does. Therefore, as he is normal he must not lift his joint properly. Just as it is abnormal for a woman to make love at 90—it is indecent, is it not? But she did.

[Moshe answers a question from a woman in the group.]

A person may forget, but the intentional cortex can reexperience or experience a possibility. I may live to be 90, but in my motor cortex there must be a representation of my shoulder because otherwise I could not move the shoulder even in the movements that I have *learned*. But we can make a new pattern of mobilization. Cells may be inhibited from the moment you are born until you're 90. A cell could be like a woman who's lived from childhood till 90, and never had a child. And the same cell will be there ready to use its potential for brain cells can not be renewed. They either live or die. Now that being so, you find that even if a person hasn't learned in 90 years, you can still make an experience to produce a pattern in which these unused cells fire. They are then integrated into their society of cells in their pattern, and fire.

Now let us continue the lesson. Would you please sit, put your right leg back, and the left forward with the left foot near your right knee. Lean on your left hand. You actually incline your body to the left. Lift your right hand in front of you, without effort. Make your wrist soft and your hand should be placed so that you can see it easily. Now turn yourself to the left the smallest amount possible where you don't feel a change of effort from the beginning of the movement. Try it a few times. Do only the movement you can do easily now. I see some hold their breath at the end. That is not the easiest movement.

Stay turned to the left, look at your hand, and now direct your gaze to your nose. See the prolongation, the extension of your nose. Suppose you had a Jewish nose, long enough to reach across the room, you could see where it would hit. Would you now lift your hand again, turn to the left to that point, wherever you feel easy, close your eyes, and move your eyes from your hand to see your right ear. While you do that, note that you think of moving your eyes horizontally to the right. Go back and forth. Make sure that you see your ear, and you don't lose the horizon. Your eyes must move very, very, slowly. When you want to focus, your eyes actually do about 200 small little movements a second. Now continue to your right ear and back again through the horizon, very smoothly, and come back to your hand, and do one more movement like that at your own pace in your own way. [To members of the group:] No, you are moving your head, move your eyes, and you're looking down, you don't look horizontally. How do I know all these things even though your eyes are closed? Miracles. Close your eyes again. Now open your eyes again and look at your hand as it is, and move your eyes horizontally, in a flicker, as far to the right as you can, and back. Now, and this time lower your hand, close your eyes, with your eyes to the front. Try to imagine how lightly you made the first part of the movement when you wanted to see your nose. That was easy. Imagine the movement lighter, so that it would be just like floating through the air.

Keep your eyes closed and lift your hand in front of your eyes. Recall the lightness, and turn to your left without changing the effort. Move with that lightness as far as you can go with eyes closed, without having to rearrange yourself to go any further. Now open your eyes, and see whether your nose has moved from the point you turned to before. Where was it before? You see, some people move very little, but some have 20, 30 and more degrees. How is that? We moved our eyes in the opposite direction, and yet this has increased the ability to turn more to the left. Now, lie on your back and see that even these few movements have made a difference in the right side from the left, from the head downwards to the foot, to the face, to the eyes.

Sit up again; in the same position as before, lift your right hand in front of your eyes, turn to the left as far as you can without any special effort, and stay there. With your eyes looking at your hand, turn your head to the right, and back again. Your eyes stay fixed on your hand as you turn your head to the right and back.

Now just think. What stops your head from going more to the right?

Continue the movement. Someone in the group is cheating, doing the movement we haven't done yet. But he can not improve his head and eyes as much, if he moves that part which I don't want to mention and ruin the lesson. Therefore, you see, if you do the correct thing right away, you've done an exercise. That's not learning. It's important to distinguish between exercising and learning, because when you do exercises you do the thing you already know; it becomes familiar and better. But it is *only* what you *know*. You have no other choice, no alternative, no improvement. What we want is an experience like a 'Eureka' experience. For that, you must turn your exercise into self-observation. Now, close your eyes, move to the middle, and then lift your right arm again in front of your eyes. Think again about the lightness of the movement and move a little bit faster. When the lightness stops, stop. [Moshé has a dialogue with a group member.] No, you close your eyes so you're not hampered by the idea of how far you've moved. If you move further, you move your hand only. (woman speaks) You move as *you;* who's you? Well, you move the whole of yourself to the left, but with your eyes closed. You're still not moving. You is only the hand, move your chest. You wouldn't have trouble with your chest if you and the chest were not enemies. The chest is *you;* it's not something you have. Alright, now go on; now you're a better chest.

Stop, open your eyes, and see whether there is an increase in the amount of rotation that you do lightly. Look now again, can you see we didn't do the exercise in the direction of movement. We moved with the eyes and the head relative to the shoulders. Take a rest and lie on your back a second. Now roll to the side, get up and sit again in the same position. (laughter) What's funny? [Question from group:] "That's a break?" [Moshé:] Yes, that's a break. If you don't believe me, try to make a break like that when you pee, and then you see whether that's a break or not. A break is just an interruption in the action; and to the brain it's an enormous relief.

Now take the same position again with your hand in front of your eyes, turn to your left as far as it feels comfortable, with your eyes open, and stay there. This time *see.* If you wish to return, notice that you must use your right hip joint. So be aware that when you turn to the left, your right buttock leaves the floor, and when you go back, your right buttock goes back to the floor. Notice too what your other leg does, and feel the change in *pressure* on your left thigh and knee. Now stay turned to the left again, and take your head and eyes back to the right. Observe: if you are very careful, you'll find that when you move your eyes and head away, you do *that* movement with your right hip joint. Now stop. Move your head and eyes as if they were frozen to your shoulders. The right hip joint must move. How does it move? Try again. Do you begin the movement with your stomach or with your back? Which lifts your right hip joint? And notice, when you lift the right hip joint, the pressure on the left increases. Therefore you do something without being aware. You didn't intend to increase the pressure on the left. But now, while you observe what you are doing, look to your left as far as you can go easily and stop. This time increase the pressure on your left hip joint and decrease the pressure on it. How do you do that? From here I can say at a mile who does it and who doesn't *think* it. If you take away pressure from your left hip joint, you'll find that your left knee moves away from the floor. If it doesn't move at all, as the Jews say, *vos a goy in klaister*! You don't know what that means?

You know that all religions love each other very dearly, because they all believe in one god. As they love themselves, therefore the Jews probably laugh at the way the Christians pray, and the Christians laugh at the way the Jews pray, with a shawl, "wawawawawawa;" it's crazy. Now we believe that what the Christians do in church is crazy, because they play music on an organ, and stand on their knees. The Jewish religion considers that ritual and ritual is anathema. If *you* don't pray to *your* god yourself then nobody does. And maybe in the Catholic religion, for instance, it's enough to confess to the priest and be relieved from your sins. The priest is representative of God. If you remember there was a time in the Middle Ages when indulgences were sold for money by the Vatican. Alright now, the pious Jews would say that if somebody was not thinking, and was not in direct connection with God, but was just doing a ritual, then that somebody was thinking now what a goy thinks in church on Monday. (laughter) Therefore you are not thinking.

Now would you please sit again and continue as before. Change the pressure on your right hip and left hip and you'll see that you will now be able to tell me how you do it. With *what* do you activate your right hip now? With the stomach muscles or the back muscles? Well, the question is idiotic, because the stomach muscles and the back muscles must work synergistically to lift the hip. Now close your eyes, sit in the middle for one second, supporting yourself with your left hand. Resume the feeling of lightness and think of both hips, and how they change while you turn. Move to your left as far as you can, doing nothing more than the lightest movement, but having in mind how the weight changes on the hips from the right to the left.

Now do one movement turning to the left to the limit of lightness. Stay there, open your eyes and see whether you have gained another 10 or 15 or 20 degrees in rotation. As you are, put your right hand on the top of your head and now you see that there is a connection between the power station and your head and eyes. If that relation is not right, the transmission of information from your head to the pelvis is not fully correct. But also the transmission of *power* from your pelvis to head is lost on the way and only a minor part of your power is useful. Stay turned to the left and with your right arm over your head bend your head taking your right ear to your right shoulder. Straighten and bend so that your left ear goes to your left shoulder. Continue to bend your head from one side to the other and now observe while you do that: does your right hip come into play, and how? Observe; when you bend your head with the left ear to the left shoulder what does the middle of the spine do? Does it move to the right or to the left?

[Moshe stops the group and asks two group members to continue the movement.] Watch and see; what is the difference in the way they do the movement from the others? Why is there no hip action? Is she more silly than you and I?

[Moshe demonstrates:] Sit; twist to the left. Put your right hand over your head and move your right ear to your right shoulder and left ear to left shoulder as most of you did a moment ago. Now the two people I had you watch did something different. They put the elbow over the forehead. Try it that way yourself and notice what happens to the movement. There is a different effect on the spine. If you want to find out why a person would do the movement that way, bend your head to the right and left with your elbow in that position, but don't move more than they did. Why is it awkward to move that way, and why did they feel comfortable in that position? Where is it awkward—with your head to the left or the right?

We will try to find out. Change to the previous position. Can you feel the difference between the two ways of doing the movement? For most people doing the movement as they did feels funny and inappropriate. Now *why* they did the movement that way we can not find out, but *how* is possible. Notice now, that using their position with the elbow over the forehead, taking the head one way results in very little movement and the other way one turns the body. If you try these movements again, you can tell by the way the spine moves which are the vertebrae that do not function normally for these two people. It is as if you had an x-ray. You can find the side, the exact vertebrae, and the organization of the intercostal and intervertebral distances.

Rest a minute; slowly roll to the side and sit again. Lean on your left hand as before, and turn to the left as far as you can go easily, moving your hips and remembering that you have shoulders, and eyes, and a head. Put your hand on the top of your head, and bend your head to the right shoulder and to the left. Now observe: when you bend your head to the left, your right side becomes longer, your chest expands, the ribs fan out, and something very curious—your right hip joint goes away from your armpit. In fact your right hip goes back to the floor to sit. Yet some people stop themselves from doing this movement; they can't bend and they can't put their left ear on their left shoulder. Try it yourself and you will see; if you don't move your right hip joint, your neck will be stiff. It's not a question of exercising. You can exercise all your life and bend your head without moving your hip. In fact that's what people do. That why they get stiff; can you imagine any animal getting stiff, as human beings get stiff when they get old? How could they lie and catch gazelles? There would be no continuing of the species. Animals get old and don't get stiff. But how? Human beings refuse to recognize that they are animals also. We say our human qualities are superior; why? Because we classified it so.

But a pigeon that homes has greater superiority in this than any human being I know; even better than Einstein. If you took Einstein in a bag, left him somewhere (laughter) and said "go home," he would be as silly as I if I were put into that bag. But you take a pigeon from a bag and the pigeon goes straight home. So you can see that if the pigeon would classify as we do, they would say: Look, the silly ass, a professor, a Nobel Prize winner, he can't go home! What do you think of a nincompoop like that? So try again taking your head to the left shoulder and right and the right side lengthens and shortens as the hip moves towards the floor and away from the floor. Stop. Return to center. Close your eyes and put your right hand in front. Turn to the left again to the point of comfort. Open your eyes, and you'll find that your nose has turned another 20 degrees to the left. This is because you now can think that the right side must get longer. We call it awareness through movement. It's not only awareness. You also get the ability to do what you want without having to exercise. What would you exercise anyhow if you don't know what you want? You can only exercise the thing you already know.

Now would you please put your hand on your shoulder, turn to the left as far as you can easily. Put your hand again on your head. You've already paid attention to the right side, take your head again to the left shoulder and now pay attention to the left side as well. On this side all the ribs go together, and the pressure of the left hip is relieved. Now watch that when you take the head to the right, the right side shrinks, and your right hip goes to your armpit. Your ribs on this side go together, and the left side gets longer; the weight shifts over your left hip joint. Continue and you will see that your pelvis rotates, and your navel moves right and left. That's true of the sex too. Because the navel cannot move away from the sex. Now you see I have a dirty mind; I think of sex all the time.

Now return to center, put your hand in front of you; just recall what you have learned, and what you felt. With your eyes closed renew the decision to turn left with even lighter movement, and when there's the slightest change, stop. Now think of your navel, and tilt to the left. Which side gets longer? Which one gets shorter? Your weight shifts to the left hip joint, to the right hip joint. Return and move to the left again and stop. And open your eyes. Have you gained another ten or twenty degrees? Do you remember how we defined learning on the first evening? We said, learning is doing the same thing in another way. Now is the rotation to the left different from your normal movement? Do you now have another way of turning to the left?

How about improving another twenty or thirty degrees? Would you please put your legs as before. [Moshé speaks to the man with hip trouble who needed support in sitting.] Watch your right hip joint—move it a little bit, turn to your left, and take it back. Can you see? You don't need an artificial hip joint, this one serves very well. (dialogue) Well, we haven't finished. When we finish, you'll have as good a hip as I (dialogue). Well I tell you: don't be bothered with time while you do it; don't succeed.

Another one of the diseases of exercise is thinking that symmetry is important. For some people doing the movement to the left and trying to do it to the right is a compulsive urge. One member of this group does it with each movement. She stops herself this way from improving the real amount that she could, and holds herself in a certain position from which she can't improve, just because of that urge. Symmetry is superficial and non-existent in any human being. In fact, the right hemisphere and left hemisphere are not the same and not symmetrical in their structure and functions. The left hemisphere contains all the things that we learned that are specifically human. This is generally true except for some left handed people. Broca's area 673, which is on the left side, is involved with speech. The left hemisphere involves writing, reading, hearing, music, for a right-handed person. These functions did not exist at birth. So everything you learn with your right hand is formed in the left hemisphere.

There was a Count of Sienna in Italy who made a challenge. He challenged anyone to walk blindfolded three hundred yards across the wide city plaza, which is paved in the old Roman way with stones, without deviating to one side or the other. Anyone who walked in a straight line like this could receive half his fortune. But no one succeeded. Now where did they land? To the right or to the left? (reply) To the right, that's correct. Similarly if you lose your way in a jungle or in a forest, and you go aimlessly, not knowing where to go, in two hours you'll be back at the place from where you started. You'll go into the forest, and keep turning to the right until you make a circle. How is this so? If you have two steel balls, one of them heavy and the other one light, and place a steel bar in between, when you move the device, the heavy steel ball will make a very small circle and the lighter ball will go around. That means the *heavy* side is the one around which we turn.

Why is the right side on the heavy side? Because your heart is only a *little* bit to your left, but the liver is the largest gland in the body and this organ sits clearly on the right side. So again you are not symmetrical.

Now what does this have to do with your symmetry? You see, if you learn actions symmetrically, you actually hamper your dominant hemisphere from doing its best. Because as soon as the dominant side turns on, you shift to the right, non-dominant hemisphere. But the right side is supposed to do a Gestalt, and the details are removed from your attention. Trying to do everything symmetrically makes us symmetrical idiots. Animals whose learning is very small compared with human learning have more symmetrical functioning in the brain that we have. Asymmetry is the essence of human superiority. As some scientists have suggested, it is the asymmetry of functioning that gives us our superiority in problem solving, and being able to think into a future situation. Now if you delay making yourself symmetrical, and leave one side as it has changed, while you walk, eat, do anything, you will feel different on that side. So you ask, why am I so clumsy in this side? In an *hour* you will have transferred learning from one side to the other, learning that can't be lost any more. This is not scholastic learning. You won't have to take an examination. But in *your* function, it is now learned as clearly as your ability to breathe.

Please put both hands to the left of your left thigh and place your weight on your hands so that there's more or less the same pressure. Pay attention to how your hips can move and look to the left with your whole body moving, including your shoulders, head and eyes. Go back again to the right, and notice that your pelvis turns so that your right buttock goes to a sitting position on the floor. Your stomach now makes a bigger movement than before, as does your pelvis. Now pay attention to your shoulders as you turn right and left. The right shoulder goes forward when you look to the left, and the left goes backwards. And when you turn back to the right your left shoulder goes forward, but the right goes right, and down, and therefore you actually round your back as if you were turning the abdomen. Going to your left, you get taller, and your head goes away from the pelvis. Now, here comes the real complication. We use something all our lives, and don't know it. We have a pelvis that moves, and shoulders, eyes, and a head that move. But observe in this movement everything is undifferentiated. All the parts move in the same direction.

Now the combination of movement possibilities are 4 multiplied by 3 multiplied by 2, or 24 possibilities. Out of those 24 possibilities the human species, without knowing, picks the ones that are easier and they learn those, and all the others are neglected over the lifespan. And people believe that they have used themselves humanly. I say they use themselves to 1/24 of their ability, which is about 5%. Observe the many movement combinations you can make with your fingers. Movements with all the fingers together are less differentiated than those in which you take three fingers one way and two another way.

For people who play a musical instrument, such as a piano or violin, the differentiation must be *enormous*. To play a series of rapid sounds requires a differentiation which is the essence of real skill learning superiority. (laughter)

Now, *look* at our body: pelvis, shoulders, eyes and neck, always go in the same direction, one of the 24 combinations possible. We will improve this later. But for now, put your right hand in front of you, close your eyes, and move to the left as far as it's easy. Now open your eyes. Move back to the place where you turned at the start of the lesson. Look how many degrees you turn now with less effort.

Now you see that the improvement you made was not through exercises, but through differentiating functions that have been undifferentiated through your adult life, for many of you since sexual maturity. If you had exercised to improve the movement for two hours, you would ache for a week. But in spite of the fatigue, in spite of the 2½ hours that you have sat in that idiotic position, when you get up you will feel lighter and better than before. So we made changes in organization that are contrary to the usual experience of the world. And this was because Functional Integration works the way the mind actually functions and sees things in another light. By comparison exercising is an idiotic habit. It has been instilled in us by the attitude of the Jewish and Christian religions.

How is that so? These religions do not permit people to enjoy life unless they pay through the nose by suffering. It is only because we sinned and were chased out of Paradise, that we have the right to exist in the first place. And that is the God we are supposed to love. (laughter) It is man's interpretation of God and it is man's interpretation of the apple and of Paradise. You can see that the whole thing is bunkum. And yet we need such religion as long as we are helpless and can't rely on our own. And we still need religion to keep us together; if we rely on our own feelings, we kill each other—worse than any other species.

If you take an experience of a species and expect to think out something new and thereby make it right, you're innocent. Modern people think that they can divorce love from sex, and that is an improvement; they don't know what sort of trouble they make for themselves. A book called *Generations and Behaviour,* shows a funny thing. If there were a compulsive habit in one generation, the next generation will take *that* habit and divorce it from the rest, and the third generation will live in doubt, and the fourth generation will do the same thing as the first generation. In Israel we have *kibbutzim*, where people tried to apply the most advanced and socialist thinking. Engineers, doctors, philosophers left everything and went to work the land, and *gave up property*. They set up an ideal Communist society where each person did the work he could do and had his needs taken care of from the common kitty of the community. There was no religion, no marriage; the children were educated by people who knew how to educate. One didn't know who the father of the child was; for they practiced free love. It is like California in the future, the *dream* of California. (laughter)

Now after 80 years of that experiment you find an extraordinary thing. The new-born young generation tells the parents: We won't be old-fashioned idiots like that. We want to be married by a rabbi. Free love is old-fashioned junk. And as the new generation was raised atheistically with free love and free everything, the parents and grandparents who never married don't really know how the children learned such values. This new generation forces the parents to marry *now*, because the Rabbinate will not marry bastards. The Rabbinate won't marry them, because they may have been non-Jewish, and therefore spoil our bank of genetic excellence. The young generation has done exactly the opposite of three previous generations.

So you can see that free love, and atheism are not as simple as people think. You can't just throw away the old junk. It's in our makeup. There's not a simple reason why people got religion. Human suffering and the difficulty of self-responsibility is part of it. Now we can only gradually change but not completely.

You saw that you improved by working asymmetrically. We did the opposite of what any normal human would do in order to move to the left. But that made it easy, because we differentiated undifferentiated functions in our nervous system. We haven't finished. Therefore the improvement you got now is only about 40%–50% of what you can do. We will continue this afternoon. Walk around. How does it feel differentiating the function a little bit more by doing practically nothing, just thinking, and talking? Find out what it feels like in the left side, and the right side. And now walk around yourself to the right, and observe how it feels. Walk around yourself to the left, and find the difference. (laughter) How would you do that with exercising? You wouldn't have learned a *tenth* of what you've learned. Thank you. (Applause. Here the lesson stops and continues in the afternoon.)

Sit with your right leg back. Lean on your left hand. Let us repeat the final parts of what we did this morning. Put both hands to your left, and lean on them properly. Remember how your head and pelvis know each other through your spine. As you start the movement turning your shoulders, head and neck to the left your pelvis moves in such a way that the weight goes to the left. On returning right you shift back to your right hip joint. Your pelvis rotates around the vertical axis a little bit. In this movement everything goes in the same direction. Now notice as your right hip joint transfers weight onto the left, one side gets longer, and allows a twisting. If you twist a thing, like a spring, then the direction of the twisting must get longer, and the other side must get pushed together. Here it is the same thing.

Now continue the movement and this time move your head and eyes in the opposite direction from your shoulders. So when your shoulders go to the left, your eyes and head go to the right and return.

This differentiated movement is unfamiliar, and unless you think it through, you can't do it. In fact you may find yourself doing the opposite and thinking that you're doing the correct movement.

Now continue until it becomes as familiar as the simple movement of your head and shoulders going together. Stop now and try the original movement with your head and shoulders together in the same direction. You will see that the movement to the right and to the left has improved. Change back to the unfamiliar movement. But note that you go more to the left *just* by differentiating the movement that you know. That's real learning; you find another way of doing what you already know. Some of the trouble that you have in your motor functions is due just to not making possible differentiations. In some cases of brain damage, you can evoke a different part of the brain to carry out a damaged function with the differentiation process.

Now stop, go back to the middle, close your eyes, put your right hand in front of you, and again make the simplest, easiest possible movement to the left, and go as far as you feel you can go without making a special effort or changing your breath. Remember, one after the other, or simultaneously, all the parts that we attended to, you'll see that the effect is tremendous. Now stop and just turn your head back to that point where it was when we started the lesson and see the difference.

Now, here we come to something which sounds crazy. Yet it is one of the 24 possibilities. Put both hands again to the left side. Now, turn your shoulders and head in the opposite direction. Now turn your eyes to the left and right as you wish; your eyes go with your head, and also with the shoulders—which is the same thing. We call that normal, which is easy, because we are so used to it and do it all the time. Now take your head and shoulders in the opposite direction. Your eyes go with your head, yes? Continue but now move your eyes with your shoulders. Slowly—if you do it fast you will make a mistake. Why is it difficult to think it through? If you check yourself, you'll see that you're probably doing one of the familiar movements. So stop and let go before you try again. Slowly continue and see whether you can get it now. Look, I turn my head and shoulders together. Now I turn my head and shoulders in the opposite direction. And now my eyes go with my head. Now I can turn my eyes in the opposite direction, and since my shoulders are turned, my eyes now turn with the shoulders. You'll see that the difficulty is in the *brain,* nowhere else. Stop and go back to the middle. Try it again. Take head and shoulders in the opposite direction, and your eyes opposite to your head but with your shoulders. Your eyes now move with your shoulders; and you *did* it, and that was easy! Why is it difficult when you want to do it at will?

Can you see? Going back to the middle was going home. Doing the movement is easy; but to do it at will is a different thing. Just like having an erection. You can do it. But do it at will now; you'll find you can't, why?

Now, now, slowly turn your head and shoulders in the opposite direction. Move your eyes in the opposite direction, and stop. You move your eyes together with your shoulders, because they are now right. Now go to the same situation from which it was easy to return home; return home, and do it again. You have learned in 20 seconds. And this is important. If you go home, you're safe. From any sort of twisted, differentiated position, you return to neutral, and the movement is easier though you move with the same coordinations. Through going home then, you learn to make the difficult combination easy. You feel you are not challenged at all. Now that's a very esoteric secret. Gurdjieff never told secrets like that to anybody. It's a secret for *everything* you want to do and can't.

And now try again. Think it through; your head turns one way, your shoulders opposite and then think how your eyes turn with your shoulders. Go slowly, and in between, return home. Try both directions. Going home doesn't mean the same thing to everybody. But it *does,* emotionally. When you get hurt or insulted, when somebody leaves you, or lets you down in a love affair, you go home to cry. It's safe there, and you can be as you like. In public the closest to home is your neutral position.

Continue until the movement of your eyes and shoulders together is perfectly easy. Stop it; move eyes and shoulders together. When you finish move your eyes to the left. Just your eyes, your head stays. Now your eyes are together with the shoulders. Stop; take your eyes and shoulders to the middle. Now you have moved the eyes together with the shoulders.

Let's try something unusual and different so that you can improve further. Put your left hand on your forehead and your right hand behind your head and roll your head between your hands.

[Moshé asks three group members to demonstrate.]

Do you see what she is doing? Can you see the difference?

[One person moves the whole body to turn while the other rolls the head as Moshé asked.]

In fact, there's no movement of her head relative to her hands at all; it was the bottom, the body, that moved. I said, "Roll your head." But people mistake a thing like that, and the mistake is so general that you can't understand how people make it. Can we say, well, they are idiots? Well, they aren't. You can find among them people who have a better intelligence than yours, except that they have their nervous system undifferentiated; they do what they *know* to do, by habit, like a bird dripping during flight. Try to roll your head. Now what's the difficulty, and why should it be so difficult as to have people move the whole body with the pelvis to do it? Now can you do both movements? Do the correct one, and the bad one. They are actually both as good as one another; they are only different ways of doing it. Now do the other one. Now you'll find that the people do the same as before. Only a minute ago you felt that you were doing it and then you lost it.

[Moshé directs a comment to a group member.]

Now, you see what you did—you're cheating; but it doesn't matter: it's better to cheat and learn than to not learn at all. Now can everybody do the two movements? Many of you will see some of the difficulties of moving your eyes with your shoulder. I'll show you in a minute why it is so difficult to do such a simple movement. And you won't believe it, because you have experienced your body for so many years, and yet none of you knows it. Notice what happens. You put your left hand on your forehead, and then you move your forehead and then your eyes move with your hand, and forehead, and head together. Everybody can do that. Therefore nobody would move the torso to do that. But now watch what happens.

[Moshé speaks to the group member he has singled out for "cheating."]

Do the movement again. Watch what he does. He actually thinks of his elbows, but he doesn't move his right hand.

Now come on, do it again. Can you see what a queer movement he does with his elbows? He has found a trick to cheat himself. But it's good; you know, he will learn the movement, because that trick will disappear in a minute. Now watch what happens now and tell me honestly who thought of it, or if anybody noticed it. As his left hand rolls his head, his hand moves right and left, and his eyes go with his hand. That's a familiar movement, isn't it? Now, I told you also to put your right hand behind your head. And now look, when you move your head to the right, your eyes and the head move in the opposite direction; that is, your eyes and head move in the same direction as your left hand but the opposite direction from your right hand. Of course this is true if you are truly rolling. But if you roll only with your left hand and not with your right, then your right hand goes the same way as your head and eyes. You have the tendency of moving both in the same direction. Did you see what he did with his elbows? I told you that's a funny thing; he tries to avoid turning his head in the opposite direction, and his elbows move in the same direction. If you roll with both hands the elbows go opposite to each other.

Now, to see what is happening—roll your head like that to the right and look with your eyes to the left when you do it. You don't understand. When I move my right hand from the right to the left, and roll, my eyes and head move from the left to the right. Both are opposite to the movement of my hand. I do the same movement and move my eyes together with my right hand; they go to the left. Such a simple thing is difficult. Your difficulty was this: every time you turned right, your eyes went right. But in order to go in the opposite direction your eyes didn't know where to go; so you moved with your body instead of your eyes. That was because you couldn't dissociate your eyes from the movement of your hand behind you.

So your eyes move to the right when your right hand goes from the right to the left. Start again; move your eyes together with your hand, as you did before. Now stop; move your eyes to the left. Now you've got it. Can you see where the difficulty was before?

Now if the rolling is clear to you, go back to the movement we did before. Put your hands to the left of your left thigh on the floor. Now turn right and left with your shoulders, eyes and head in the same direction. Your eyes move with your head. Now slowly, move your eyes with your shoulders and your head as before in the opposite direction. Stop; stay there; lift your right hand in front of your eyes as before and twist yourself to the left. See how far you go now. You are now investigating how not to be stiff with old age. Many people stop using their brains in any other situation than the one which was familiar to them from early childhood. They made only one combination possible, and that becomes so exclusive that considerable parts of the brain are inhibited. Neurons have never fired in any other pattern. Now some people die and you can transplant their liver or heart or kidneys which still function quite well. Which part then died? Those parts of the brain that have never worked. They become sclerotic. The person may have been completely dotty, since some parts were used completely and others weren't used at all. What was not used is dead and unable to move. Some old people can remember clearly what happened 25 years ago, but can't tell you what happened yesterday or a minute ago. Or someone tells you a story and two seconds later he tells you the same story again. That's putting it of course in a very general way; it's not as simple as that. But as a first approximation we can say we get dotty, because we use one pattern and use that until it's exhausted.

Let's see, this time have you reached the limit of your ability? Put both hands a little more to the left, and move your eyes and head and everything to the left; see whether you can see straight back. But you could see *another* 90 degrees. Here's a person who complained that her right hip was wobbly; watch what she does with her right hip now. She can see the window, and has turned 70 degrees. And here someone can see the corner of the other window. Therefore she turned slightly over 270 degrees.

Now go back to where you turned easily at the very beginning. Go just short of where you go easily now. Have you increased your turning angle five or six times? But we did nothing, except differentiate some parts of the eyes and the head. Now would you please lie down and rest a little.

Learning is the kind of process where you learn to do the thing you can do in a different way, so that your choice is increased. The difference must be significant. Otherwise your choice isn't free. No one forces you to do this movement or that movement. But you have your free choice.

You can see we have postponed doing the other side completely; we acted asymmetrically. It's a wonderful experience nevertheless. You feel that half of you is good and the other half is as you came here. It is clumsy and does not obey you.

On the left side you are there and you know it. On the right side you are as you were. You do not know your ability and have no sense of the differentiation. So please sit with your left leg back, lean on your right hand, close your eyes, and lift your left hand. Imagine only that you will turn to the right. And now imagine that you're going to move your eyes in the opposite direction to your left. Move a tiny little bit to the right, and in this position move your eyes to the left in your thought only, and see your left ear. Let your breathing be shallow, undisturbed by your thoughts. And now think that you move your eyes to see your left ear, but in such a way that your eyes glide along the horizon uniformly. You'll find that it is not possible to do absolutely nothing. If you have the intention to move, the organization is already present, and you can feel actually that your muscles respond to your thought even if you don't make an extensive movement.

Now lower your hand, for a brief rest. Lift it again. This time close your eyes again, and you'll move your head to the right as far as you can go without effort, in your imagination. Now as you think the movement, can you feel it in your left hip joint? Do you think of making an effort, or are you just gliding to the position? Are you getting stiff in your chest or spine as you imagine? Would your left hip actually leave the floor and the weight go over to the right hip joint? Lift your hand in front of you and close your eyes, and then do it in the slightest possible way. Turn to the right and find out where you can turn effortlessly. Stay there, open your eyes, and have a look. It's more effective than actual movement from the very start. You just imagined two movements—look how much you turned.

Put your left hand in front of you again and now move to the right as far as you can go gently, comfortably. Close your eyes, and move your hips mentally, in your imagination, thinking that you sit back on your left buttock. You have to restrict yourself to think. You must organize the intention to act, but you don't use your muscles extensively or the joints. It's a question of movement in your brain.

As you continue, you'll see that your right knee must lift. What do you have to do with your shoulders and your head? Do five or six movements mentally. In order to think the movement, you have to feel your weight lean on your right shoulder, and that you actually push your body so that your spine lengthens and your head becomes taller. As you then move to sit on the left hip, you push your shoulder away from your right hand. Now just represent the movement in your imagination.

Stop; come back to the front; put your left hand in front of you, and with closed eyes do the easiest, lightest possible turning movement to the right. How much have you gained? It's incredibly more effective to think than to work and actually do the movement. All right now, take your hand in front of you again, turn to the right as far as you go easily. Put your left hand on top of your head. Remember, if you bend your head with the left ear to the left shoulder, then your left buttock should lift. The left side gets shorter. Just think how your left hip joint goes towards your left armpit, and how the whole left side will shrink like an accordion, and then open up like a Japanese fan. Think how you bend your head to the left to do that, and then right, and then observe something that you probably didn't notice before. If you bend your head to the right in your imagination, then the ribs on the right side of your chest will move away from your right elbow. Bend it in actuality once, and you'll see that it *is* so. Then you can think it. As you bend find out how much the gap increases between your right arm and ribs. Now put your hand on top, and *imagine* that gap. As you imagine that gap, you can also imagine your left buttock touching the floor. You'll also feel that your right thigh tends to go up and therefore your stomach muscles begin to twitch as if they are going to do something. Continue thinking that you take your right ear to the right shoulder, and your left to the left, and increase the movement in your imagination. As you do this observe all the things that you should be feeling; for example, the increase and decrease in the gap, the shortening of one side as the other side lengthens, and so on. Then turn back to the front, lift your hand in front of you, and as easily as you can, turn to the right, and see. But think of all the things that you felt. See how *effective* thinking is! You will achieve more with less effort, and the muscles on that side will not be tired. Therefore the movement will be incomparably lighter than the other side, though we haven't done a thing at all, and will do it in a tenth of the time.

Well, now close your eyes. Put both your hands to your right side, and this time think of the distance between your tail and the top of your head. If you want to turn a little bit right, what does your pelvis do, your navel, your legs? Just think of it. Think that you're going to move your shoulders, head and eyes together. Now move your shoulders and head in the opposite direction three times in your imagination so that as your shoulders move to the right, your head and eyes go to the left. Now your eyes can go together with your head, to the left, and they can go to the right together with your shoulders.

Now think, when you move your head in the opposite direction, what you do with the eyes. You decide: will you move them with the shoulders, or with the head? And I say that if you think that thought through, whether you succeed or not, just attempting to differentiate the movement, you will find a major improvement. If you now try to turn to your right you won't believe how far you will go. Leave your hands as they are, look to the right and see how far you can go and then see how you can turn to the front. Look what sort of twist you achieved here, doing nothing.

Stop and sit; which side feels better? Change over your legs. As you sit to the other side, twist yourself to the left and find out how it feels. Go where it's easy, and you'll be able to tell the difference. Change over again and try the other direction. Find which side is easier to turn with both hands on the floor. Which is easier; the one we worked hard with, or the one we imagined? Change over again, until you can equalize both sides.

Now think of the easy side, and make the other side easier. As you do that, the corpus callosum, which includes a few billion fibers, connects the right hemisphere with the left. Thus everything that one half of the brain and one half of the body has learned to do, transfers to the other side. This is the kind of learning that makes a man into a human genius. It gives you the right to call yourself a human being. You are no longer limited to one combination out of 24 possibilities and pass all your life doing that one idiotic thing.

Change over your legs, one side and the other. Think that you turn more easily. Imagine the movement in your arse, your feet, your pelvis, your stomach, your shoulders, your front, your neck, your eyes. Go right and left, wherever you like. Your shoulders can go with your eyes, or without your eyes. As you continue, you get taller, and wider.

And now go ahead and have a look. How far can you see? Stop; if you can see to the limit by lifting, you can do it also without lifting. It's enough to imagine it now. You'll find that every auxiliary movement we do is only to facilitate learning. After we learn we can do without it. Now you'll see that you

can see the window without lifting your weight. Make yourself
longer. What part gets stiff? That's the part that needs to stop
working. That's it. To go that far you thought that you must
lift yourself off the floor. Don't make your trunk stiff relative
to your pelvis. There is no limit to imagination in thinking. If
there were limits, you wouldn't be able to fly from here to
Tokyo; we wouldn't have Telstar and we wouldn't go to the
moon. In other domains we are still keeping one pattern of the
whole 24 possibilities. Especially as far as social organization
goes, and government and taxes. . . . We keep the old-fashioned
idiotic way of thinking and consider it religion. Even the President has to pay tribute; he must show that he goes to church
on Sunday, otherwise he wouldn't be a president. Now I have
nothing against going to church on Sunday, if it is a free
choice. But it is not our free choice. Inflation, pollution, and
similar problems exist because we have one silly pattern of
using ourselves and we do not allow ourselves to change. For
some people it takes five centuries to realize that if you shit
everywhere in the sea, the sea will be polluted with shit. The
Mediterranean has 12 cities that have more than 2 million
people, and they all pollute. How long can the sea be clean?
If you look at that, you can see it is the patterns that were
never challenged and are adopted and continued that keep us
away from being responsible human beings that do the best for
ourselves.

Now get up and find out what it feels like. Walk around.
Now twist yourself to look backwards or sideways as you walk.
Do it as if you were backing a car. You can look straight
backward and walk without any difficulty. Look forward, and
look backwards on the other side. Some elderly people can
only look in the mirror; they cannot look backwards when
they drive a car—they can now. How could you expect a whole
group of old people, fat people, young people, and bearded
people, to learn that so easily? Can you see that the learning
is *general;* it's not the cleverest who learns; it's not the best
pupil in the class who is good. Everyone has improved. I think
that is real *learning.* Let us take a break. (applause)

LESSON EIGHT:
THE SEVENTH CERVICAL

Please stand on your knees. Put the back of your right hand into your left palm, and place them on the floor in front of you; place your forehead into your hands. Now would you please rock your body with your pelvis, forward and backwards. Observe what you do, and what happens to the rest of your body. Now note, when you go *forward,* does the middle of your spine go nearer to the floor, or away from the floor? Can you feel which vertebrae go away from the floor? And do you draw your stomach in? And where do you round your spine? Which vertebrae get rounded?

Go slower. Now imagine, you know where your anus is. Go from the anus to your spine and note which vertebra is the first to go up when you go forward. Most people have five lumbar vertebrae. Which vertebra behind your chest goes the highest? You have three floating ribs. Is the last of the floating ribs moving upwards or isn't it? Does that part of your back round as you continue the movement? When I ask, I don't expect an answer. I know the answer. So keep it to yourself. Between your shoulders, you have a large vertebra behind the seventh cervical. Many people have a lot of fat around it and it's very awkward for them. When you do the movement now, does this vertebra move somewhere? Can you feel that the shoulder blades go together as you go back and when you go forward the shoulder blades go apart? Many people have no idea that that can happen. And they can't do it unless they make tremendous idiotic efforts.

Now make your breathing shallow and *don't* push that vertebra so that you won't be able to move afterwards. Make a small movement so that the spine between the shoulder blades goes forward and back, but not to the limit of your ability, but to just the beginning. Then you have a chance to find out what it feels like and improve it.

Now, move your pelvis forward, so that the middle of the spine between the shoulder blades moves *more* forward and the shoulder blades *remain* so that you feel that the spine between your shoulder blades has moved forward. *Stay* there; then collapse the spine so that it falls in between the shoulder blades, and the shoulder blades join to touch one another. You can't do that?

Stop; lie on the floor on your stomach. Now put both elbows on either side of your body as if you were to stand on them. Both hands are forward like a dog or a sphinx. Your shoulders stand over your elbows. That's what a dog would do, because he's intelligent. The elbows should be not too near, not too far. You must judge for yourself. It should feel that you could support someone on your shoulders.

Now look up to the horizon, and sink your spine in between your shoulders and join the shoulder blades. Push the floor with your elbows, so that your shoulder blades move apart and your spine lifts. Your head lifts with your spine, but stays fixed in relation to your spine so that your eyes continue to look to the horizon. There's one correct place for your elbows. Can you feel it?

Try putting your elbows too far forward and then too far back until you find the place that is right for yourself. Here your elbows can stand and support weight, so your muscles have nothing to do, only hold. Your hands lying on the floor hold your shoulders in the right way. Now, look at the horizon and *sink* between your shoulders. Don't change the way your head looks at the horizon. Continue to go in and out with your spine until you stop intervening with the rest of the body. Now sink and get up, only with your right elbow. Your left elbow makes no pressure on the floor. Now continue with your left elbow making the sinking movement; the right one stays where it is with no pressure underneath. Now with both arms together sink and lift. Observe! Which vertebra goes forward more than any other? Which goes higher to the ceiling? You won't be able to tell if you allow your chin to move nearer, because another vertebra will move more forward or higher.

Now would you please look at the ceiling, and sink and get up. Can you see? It's the shoulder blades that go together and apart, and the shoulders go narrower and wider. Look at the horizon, and look at the ceiling. That's enough. Stop for a minute. Get up and walk around, and observe what you feel. Where is your head in space as you walk? How is your breathing? And the width of your shoulders?

Now lie on your back. Lift your head to look at the horizon with your shoulder blades, and take your elbows back, so that you can lean on your elbows. With your legs extended let your feet lie sideways, open like that. Look at the horizon in front of you, and sink between your shoulder blades and get out again. Don't change the position of your head. It's your arms, shoulders, shoulder blades, and clavicles that now move the spine. Now observe which is the vertebra that is actually being pushed out forward. Do it several times. Observe that your head goes away from your pelvis and gets higher when you do that. Now observe what you do with your pelvis. Do you have to lift your back from the floor? Certainly not. Make five movements each simpler than the other.

And now don't move your spine or anything else, but move both shoulders forward and both shoulders backward. Does your spine sink in between or not? Now if you move your shoulders backward, sink with your spine in between. *Stay* there, sunk like that, and move your shoulders forward and backward. You will find you can't move them forward and backward unless your head gets a little bit taller. Now, move them forward more, and backwards and forward. Take your shoulders to the middle, and keep them there. Sink in between and get out. Notice what your forehead does. If you have to make movements with your stomach and chest, stop. We only want the sinking movement. For many people it's very difficult to do; some people strain their backs and don't realize it. This happens because the distance increases between your back and the floor. Therefore you're not sinking. Now you have to be able to do the wrong thing and the right thing before you can be correct. If you can't tell lies, you can't tell the truth. Only sink between your shoulders and get out. Some still strain the back. So as you continue, think of contracting your chest and upper back. That's what you're actually doing. There is almost no sinking movement when you contract like that. Think of your head: the forehead goes forward and upwards; the top of your head goes up. You don't need your back at all. Imagine that you have a grapefruit on your head, and make sure that it cannot fall. Sink and get up, and then your back won't do the work. Can you feel the difference?

Now try again, and strain your back so that your stomach gets stiff. Do it the wrong way. Now do it without strain, just with the shoulders alone. Your head gets taller. Unless you make the mistake and get rid of the mistake, you can't really learn. The initial learning of the human species is done in that way, i.e., eliminating the things that are useless for the activity. A baby does not learn to do something right, because he doesn't know the purpose of it. He only moves and when something interferes with his action, some parasitic, useless thing, he stops doing that. He discovers; hu-hu. That's it. Wonderful. That's how he learns to walk. Therefore when you eliminate the parasitic, useless movements that you enact, that's learning. We said that yesterday. A child with cerebral palsy can't learn, because he doesn't know the parasitic movement. Every time he tries, it's *another* useless action, because his condition is erratic. Therefore he hasn't got a movement to eliminate, and doesn't know what to do. He can't get any better. Now you should have the ability to eliminate useless, parasitic, superfluous rubbish. Then you can have a clear vibrating voice.

Stand again on your knees and your hands. Put your left

hand into the right hand, and put them on the floor. Put the place where your hair grows (hairline) in to your hands, and now sink in between your shoulders and get out of it and see the difference; compare what you did before and what you do now. The middle of your spine and sternum should move. Take your shoulders apart so the middle can sink. [To someone in the group:] No, you see you move your shoulders forward and you make a different movement of your spine, *only* because you move your chest. There is no differentiation. Now instead of sinking, do that; take the shoulders forward. That's not sinking; but some people mistake that for sinking. Take them backwards. This is a different movement. Now go right and left; the shoulder blades go *away* from one another. For some people it is as difficult as dying. [Moshé asks the group to watch four group members who carry out the movement in different ways.] Look how much sinking there is between her shoulders and what does she do with the rest of the body and the head, and the arse? Now look here, no movement of the arse. But here, the shoulders go apart; in all the others the shoulders do such idiotic things. He has to change the pelvis a little bit, because he has never learned to differentiate his spine all along. [Moshe speaks to one person specifically.] Can you see that now you move your shoulders? You still move them forward. Do it as you did before, what felt comfortable. No, you see, you move forward and backward, and the spine doesn't sink, because it's still round, and look, it's specially round on the right side of your chest. You're still moving it forward unnecessarily. That's better, take both shoulders sideways. Look, it's very difficult, as she has never done it before.- Now let's correct all the mistakes you saw; only then you'll find what is the right thing to do. First, try all the mistakes the others did. To learn to move as the people who do it wrongly is more instructive than doing the right thing. The right thing becomes more right by eliminating all sorts of useless junk. Now if you can do the wrong thing you can do the right thing.

Now sit down; I'll tell you a story, so that you can laugh.

The Theosophical Society thought that they could save the world by looking for a savior the way the Tibetans search for a Dalai-Lama. There are rules in Tibet and in other places to find the place where a guru or king of the earth will be born using the stars, and so on.

Now the Theosophical Society did the same thing, and their sages found a very poor Indian, who had eight or ten children. One child was the right one. They took that child to educate him to be the head, the new messiah, the person that would change the world. He would see an end to wars, and would be able to use the resources of the world to improve the world. That child was Krishnamurti. When they tried to take him he made a fuss and wouldn't go. He wouldn't leave his brother. The others didn't matter, but there was one brother he held to, so they took two brothers. They raised Krishnamurti and educated him to be the leader of the world. He was sent to Oxford and he learned Chinese and was educated to be a superior human being. When he was 18, the Theosophists gathered in Ceylon from the world over to *crown* Krishnamurti to be the leader. They gave him the money to be able to reorganize a better world.

You see, all those people believed that if they have the right ideas about how people should live among themselves and if they provided the money to organize that, then it would be done. Now, Krishnamurti, who was educated to learn the truth (he had extraordinary tutors) and was a very extraordinarily bright person, got up and said to them, I refuse to be the leader of the best Society that can improve humanity. It is because *you,* who believe you're doing the right thing, actually believe that you're better than any other human being and can teach other human beings how to be good human beings. But if you believe that you're superior to all the others, the others will refuse to learn from you; they will hate the sight of you. You believe that you are the best people in the world, and you know the secret of how the species should live.

Well, I believe that you are egotistic, superior nincompoops, because you're not better than the other people, you're in fact worse. You already consider that your Society is the best, and if Societies would have to be like you are now, it would be a disaster.

He said, this is the source of war. This is the source of inequality in the world. If some people teach others, they think that they're superior. But you're only a human being like the others; therefore teach yourself; don't teach anybody else; use the money to improve yourself. I won't have anything to do with people who're so bigotedly right and superior to anybody else. One of the main teachings of Krishnamurti is: don't teach, learn. And actually he had a lot of trouble in his life, a lot of failure too. I believe that Krishnamurti is an extraordinary human being, and if you read some of his books, you will be thrilled to find a human being who doesn't teach you, but you can learn from him. He gives you only his own experience, and asks you to consider it, that's all. He doesn't tell you: do that or don't do that. Now here we do the same thing. To perceive what is right you must do the wrong thing. So try now to repeat every mistake you saw. [Moshé now points out the details of how a number of the group members accomplish the movement, and asks the group to watch each one.] Can you see? Watch her chest, spine, and pelvis, and note how her head rocks with her chin downwards. Now if you watch others you see the pelvis move, but here's someone who doesn't sink but goes forward, his chin rocks and his shoulders move forward and backward, but they don't move right and left.

Here she does move her pelvis, but her shoulder blades go up and down, backwards. And the part of her spine that goes out is below the shoulder blades. Now here is someone who moves the shoulders more forward than sideways, and here is someone who practically doesn't move her pelvis. Try many variations. Try different positions of your elbows making them wider and more narrow.

[Moshe directs remarks to one group member.] Put your elbows where you wanted them in your own way. Now sink between your shoulders. In the first movement you did you made an effort with your stomach muscles that was not necessary. Now that you've stopped, watch: your shoulders move apart only, and do not move forward and backward. And your spine goes up, just in the middle of your shoulders. That's the seventh cervical vertebra which moves. Now hold my finger with your shoulder blades. [Moshé places his fingers between the shoulder blades in the back.] Take them together, squeeze my hand: take them apart.

[Moshé tries the same procedure with another person.] Now would you do it. Watch, there is practically no movement here. Squeeze your shoulders and hold my hand. Watch, he pushes it out, and they're so close that there is no room for my fingers. Now take them apart. He takes them apart less than she.

But that will improve; it is just the beginning.

Each one of you continue now, and go slowly and gently so that you can eliminate all the junk that you don't want. You can reorganize yourself only when you do it gently, slowly, and don't try to be correct. There's no harm in doing a movement in any way. But there is very large harm for yourself, if you don't use all that you could to a higher degree of perfection, and satisfaction to yourself.

Make a small movement, so that you can be sure that your shoulders go only together and apart. Now you're sinking. And when you will succeed, you will realize how much more beautiful you are. When you get up you'll have another face, and another head, and another pair of shoulders.

Stop; get up and find out what it feels like in your shoulders, your body, all of you. Observe how you hold your shoulders and your head.

Are you doing something you've never done before? Can you notice that you stand in a way that is unfamiliar to you? The balance of your head and body and shoulders is different from your habitual way. Now walk around a little bit, and notice what it feels like. Move your shoulders forwards and backwards. Your shoulder blades go together and apart. Forget it. Laugh a little. I am ready actually to have a rest. Thank you. (applause)

Discussion: Trying to Forget

Would you please try to forget what we did from the first day until today, and see if by trying to forget, you can at least have an idea of all that we did. You remember what we started with? Then forget it if you don't remember. Try to forget what you don't remember. And what did we do yesterday? Now there shouldn't be much difficulty. What did we do yesterday afternoon? Does anybody remember that damn movement sinking between your shoulders? (laughter) Now there's a-nother means of remembering: that is to do it as an exercise, and do it 50 times, and then rest, and do it another 50 times. Then you'll remember it at least a fortnight, because it will be painful to get up in the morning. So that's one way of remembering. How did we arrive at that movement of sinking the spine in between the shoulders? Remember, we did it in two ways: on your back and on your stomach. But why did it come to my mind to present that lesson, and why suddenly yesterday, why not before yesterday? Can you see any connection between what we did and the question that was asked about the eyes? Do you remember the answer, and how we viewed the body in terms of the power of the pelvis? We showed that the pelvis is more powerful than the fingers, toes, elbows, and knees, and that the pelvis contains the largest muscles including the gluteals, the quadriceps, the lower stronger abdominal muscle. And then we saw a head was like a safe in which something is kept so that even the person himself can't touch it, because it's so precious. We found that the head and pelvis are so structured in the nervous system, that if the one doesn't connect to the other, then your power can not be used for your intention. Can you see, it was not by chance that we did that. What's the purpose that *you* feel in it? Look, if I can not move my spine and shoulders then my head is restricted, and if somebody calls me here I am not prepared and therefore how can I respond to a movement there? By the time I am doing that, it's all over isn't it?

So why do the lesson turning with your hand in front of you? To make it possible for your head to scan the entire horizon. And why did you differentiate your eyes? So that you can turn easily. It's just like riding on a bicycle between two cars—you have to look right and left while moving forward, and attending to your balance. The pelvis goes straight away; it's the power station that moves you forward. But the information and the intention where to go depends on the cars on either side. For that you must move your eyes. You may even have to move your head here and eyes there. If you're really moving, and don't do that, you will not survive five seconds. We called that differentiation. Therefore what we did all through the day had one straight line of thought: answering your question about the eyes.

Very few people go beyond the normal development and learning that happens from childhood until we are sexually mature. We think we are already perfect because we have learned the one possibility out of 24—only eyes, head, shoulders, and pelvis together. The entire day yesterday we harped on that theme, working with it in successive approximations —answering the question that wasn't asked: why is there a relation between the eye and the head? But the question itself shows the infantile development of the whole group, myself and everybody else included. Before you have the idea that it is one of 24 possibilities, nobody bothers about it. In a Catholic house you learn the Catholic religion, and ignore all the others; they're of no importance. And in the Jewish home it is exactly the same thing; in the Moslem home it's the same thing. But if you want to know more, if you want to be human, you must find that not only is it the Moslem and Jewish religions that have one God, but other religions have nothing to do with God at all. Real Buddhism has nothing to do with God. Buddha himself didn't talk about God. He talked about a way of life that makes your misery comfortable. He was a prince, and had a child and a beautiful woman, and the moment the child was born he left. He spent many years in a hole in the earth, thinking, why he does suffer, and why is he afraid of death, and why is the child going to die? He gave you a way of life that had nothing to do with God. But some of his followers tied it to God. There's even a follower in Switzerland who shows that yoga and Buddha are the same as the Christian religion.

So when you think about what is religion, you'll find that there is Lao Tze, Shinto, Confucius, Zarathustra, and the Egyptians with their Appis and the Golden Ox. When you look at it, how many religions are there? And out of all of them only one is familiar.

The same here: from all the possibilities, we know one. Now what do you remember? It's easy to remember because there is interconnection. Without a sense of a sensible, intelligent interconnection, you can't remember any details. Is there anybody who doesn't remember that seven is after six, or that 93 is after 92? Why? Because there's a sense in that. But if you take all the numbers, write them on cubes, and throw them out and then take out 87, is it before 92 or after 92? You wouldn't know. Because there's no sense in that. You know only when I ask you, but not if you took a cube and the cubes are dispersed and just in a heap, each one bearing a number. In other words: it's only because we have a natural serial number progression that you can find any number, place it where it is; we wouldn't if we didn't know that; and in fact if you ask some primitive people who haven't been to school, you will see what sort of things they produce when they calculate. They use other means.

When I was a *halutz*, a worker, we lived in tents on the sand. The Arab population was on one side and the Jewish was on the other. In the middle in a few hundred yards of sand we were building. We bought what we needed from an Arab there. I learned that *bethojan* means eggplant, and how to say in Arabic, *chtiar*, *muchalem*. Chtiar is pickles. The Arab didn't know to write or read, but was very intelligent. He had a clientele of 50 Jews and about 200 Arabs who used to come to him and pay him at the end of the month. Now everybody in our modern society would write it down, if he or she gave credit. But he couldn't write. What did he do? Let us say that the man with the moustache got pickles on Friday last and at the end of the month said, "Can't be that I owe you 70 piasters." The Arab would reply, "Look, at the first week of the moon you came here on Tuesday and you got bananas, and you got pitas, and it was 17½ piasters, and then the next week—at the quarter of the moon you got pickles and eggplant—and you owe me 97 piasters." He could do that with everyone who came in the place, and with whom he gave credit. He could tell them where they came from, how they were dressed, and with whom they came. He never made a mistake. And it was done without knowing how to read and write. How did he do it? He had clues that escape our notice. You would never think of that.

Now you can see that our simple way of doing things is not as simple as it looks. We spoke about how we use our eyes to see a constant world and how we move our eyes and head and body together. But I can tell you that the Bedouins and Yemenities don't learn to read as we do. As there's only one Koran in the hands of the teacher, and not every child can afford to buy one. Of all the things that we learn, they learn at least two combinations, not one. I was first struck with this fact riding on a train. A Yemenite man with a face of a Jesus, a beautiful, intelligent, and benevolent face, sat with me. You could see he was a cultured man. He held a book upside down; turned a page. As he appeared very interested, he obviously was reading. I looked at him and I thought: the man is either cuckoo, or I can't understand what he's doing. I had to ask him, "Can you read?" He said, "Don't you see I'm reading?" I said, "But how are you reading? You're holding the book upside down." He said, "What do you mean upside down? Which is the right side up?" So I thought I was dealing with somebody who came from Mars. He saw that I couldn't understand and he laughed. "We Yemenites lived in the desert. We had no more than one Bible in the town where we lived, and all the children had to learn to read and write. So our teacher had a book, and the children would sit around. He would hold and show: *bereshit bara Elohim*, at the beginning God created. Each one would see the book from another angle, and as they changed places at different times each would learn to read from every angle. For us there is no upside down, no side at all." Then he explained to me, "You European people are cuckoo, when you can read a book only from one side. I can't understand it," he said. "You look like intelligent people. You go to universities, and can read a book only in one way. Look, that book now, turn it in any way you like, I can read it, it's the same, "ee" and "oh" from any side. It's the pattern of the "ee" that you recognize." For us that is completely unthinkable. But if you try it, you'll see that you can learn to read from any side.

Now you see, of all the combinations possible we've picked one, making a book with one side up and down, and we can't read it in any other way. I would have to train a month to read as he did. He gave me the book and asked me to turn it as he continued to read. Provided I didn't turn it too fast, he continued reading, all the time while I was moving. There was no difficulty for him. His eyes would follow the line. Now he never went to the university, nor to high school. But since we only choose one out of 24 possibilities, can you see that some primitive people are better than we are? Primitive? Or are they really cultured people and *we* primitive, because we haven't made the differentiating that they have?

Alright, can you now remember what was our motive for learning the day before? Don't remember details, but can you think what we did? Can you see the difference between exercises and learning for the sake of finding another way of doing a thing that we already know? For us it's so difficult. We dedicate time and money to learn, and yet two minutes, an hour later, we haven't got the faintest idea what we have done, nor any idea of what we have learned; why is that so? Because the average human being, in our culture, is unable to fix his attention on something for more than three-quarters of an hour usefully. If he does more than that daily he just stuffs himself like someone overeating. The brain gets overfed, and therefore unable to digest anything. You see, Gurdjieff said the mind, our brain, our whatever it is, is just like the digestive function. We eat the same things, which contain a lot of nutrients, yet we grow very differently. When we eat food we first select what we eat, break it down with the violence of our strong teeth, then assimilate what we can out of it, and throw away what is impossible to assimilate.

Now learning is exactly the same thing. When you learn something, either you can digest it or you can't. Part almost everyone can digest. But the part that a person assimilates depends on one's mental health and on the method of learning. Just as in feeding—you can feed so that it's harmful to one —learning can be more harmful. Now learning what is useful depends upon what you can assimilate into your own previous structure and understanding. You must also be capable of throwing away the useless parts. Just as in eating, learning requires digestion. In learning you find things that you *can* assimilate easily, and some that you reject. There are things I say that you don't even know that I said later. But we have my words recorded. That happens with anybody in learning. In my graduate course the things that I said the first year my students didn't remember when I repeated them the third, or the fourth year. Now, if we *do* learn too much you find the learning marvelous and new, but in the end you don't know. Luckily, our system is so made that in spite of that we retain something. But did you notice what we did to remedy that general inability to learn?

In everything we did, we tried to structure it in such a way that you could not help but look at the thing you could digest, and then get up and find out what could you throw away. So we did a lesson on one side and let you do the other side without doing. Whatever we did it was not the exercise that was important, but what people got in their way of understanding and getting a new way of learning. They learned whether they understood in words or not. Therefore the improvement was general. But it wasn't an accident, although it looked like it was just fun. The lesson was like beads on a string; you couldn't take off a bead without destroying the string altogether. If you look from the first moment we started until now, there was not a bead that was displaced before the other bead. That means we never tore the string on which the beads were put. And if you don't feel that string, you will find that you have to write notes. If you don't have the string, the beads are a mess. If you don't have that natural sequence of numbers, then if you put the numbers just haphazard, you have to be a world genius to find that 87 is before 92. It isn't always so; it's only when there is a *string* on which they are put.

The movements we did are the same. You cannot remember unless you know the string. I tried to make that string quite clear all the time. Now that you know that it's a string of beads, you'll find that probably what we do *now* you will remember much better than what we did yesterday. That's how we are constructed.

Well now, can you now try to forget what we did the first day after the introduction of learning? And the next morning, what was the first thing we did? By the way, did you notice the first time I asked questions about a lesson I asked, what is the thing you disliked? Why? I wanted you to become aware that learning also means rejecting what you can't assimilate at the moment. No one who heard the first evening introduction did not find some places in which he or she felt doubt or said, "Oh, it's quite right what he says—he is quite right." And therefore my first question was, what was the thing you threw away from what you heard? My next question was, what was the most pleasant thing? These were beads on the string. So there was no question of which question was the first. Now can you find any of the beads in your own way from the first evening? What is the sequence of lessons that we have done? Whether it's correct or not is not important. And don't be so serious. If you are too serious it means you are trying to do it the way you did it before. Then you think, if you fail you're no good. And he remembers, she remembers, and you don't. Therefore you continue building your inferiority and in fact you don't rely on yourself and don't build up your power of responsibility and self-esteem. As we've trained like that all our lives, so you cannot change it in three days. Therefore here it doesn't matter at all if you don't remember a thing.

And now that you're not supposed to remember, you'll see that something comes to your mind anyway. You can't forget *all* the things. Do you recall that I gave you five seconds, and actually *told* you what you had to try to remember? I gave you the first day, and all the data; I asked you to recall the lesson, I told you what you're asked to recall. But I didn't challenge you and didn't ask you to repeat anything. You could be relaxed and didn't need to remember. Everyone smiled and felt that he really knew it.

Alright, now I *challenge* you to do it the way you want, remember or don't, to recall or not. You'll see that when everybody gets laughing about it and is not really tense in order to recall, there are many things that come to the mind quite easily. And once you learn that you'll find that there's no difficulty at all in recalling most of the things, no difficulty.

LESSON NINE:
HEAD THROUGH THE GATE

Would you please stand on your knees, put your hands on the floor, and very slowly move your pelvis backward as if to sit on your heels. But don't sit; make a small movement, and return. Do that several times. Now if you care to have a look around yourselves you'll see that most people have their heads in the same relative position to each other. Now of course if you lift it, you'll find everyone lifting. (laughter)

Now would you please slide—in mechanics we say translate —your pelvis to the right. When you slide the pelvis, there is no turning, but the pelvis moves parallel to itself. At the beginning you move as you can. Move your pelvis to the right, and back again. As you do that, you stand on your right knee. You'll find that most people are not able. Now would you please join your knees and move the pelvis to the right. No difficulty; most people can do that quite easily. Now move it both to the right and left, as it is, and observe; when you go to the right, you stand on the right knee; when you go to the left you stand on the left knee.

Now lift the knee that is useless as you shift. Can you see now the movement is peculiarly different? Lift the left knee, and then go back and lift the right, keeping your knees as close together as possible. Don't move it to the side, just lift off the floor. Now go ahead, accelerate that movement, gently. Observe only how many of you move your head right and left. But one person moves her head right and left an amount which is greater than everyone else. And that's the person who couldn't sink between the shoulder blades. She could not move her shoulders apart, but did some sort of funny movement in order to get up.

Move your pelvis as fast as you can. Now watch: should your head move? Now stop. You move your pelvis fast; is your arse and the head the same thing? Why is your head stationary? Well, when you move fast, it should be stationary; it's only when you move the whole body that it is not stationary. For the movement of your pelvis right and left, your head is stationary; the faster you go the more stationary it is. Do the movement again, and move your head and shoulders together. When your pelvis goes to the left, your head goes to the right. Now obviously, you're turning the whole body. In other words, to you, turning the pelvis means turning the body. Now go ahead, right and left, and now try to lift the knees one after the other, and go faster, and your head won't move even if you want it to.

Stop a minute. Now try again; put your hands on the floor, and open your knees as wide as you can. As wide as you can means as wide as you can humanly, otherwise you'll find that you'll not be able to move after that. This time slide your pelvis to the right. Ha, you see it's difficult. Move your pelvis to the right, to the middle, and back again; but don't rotate the pelvis; just put the weight on the right leg, so that you can lift the left knee a tiny bit off the floor. You should be able to stand on your right knee. It's not easy, and if you succeed at it at once, you'll do it certainly in a way which is not useful to you.

Continue and bang your knees as you did when your knees were together. Lift your right knee and bang it to the floor, and then the left. Any one who put his legs *wider* than he can actively use them will find it extremely difficult to do.

Observe how much rotation you do with the pelvis while doing that. You see, some can't do it otherwise than by rotating the pelvis, and some can. Now put your knees together again, and shift the weight onto the right knee or the left and notice the lightness of the movement. That lightness should persist even when you open your knees a little more. Do that and observe that that is correct.

Stop banging your knees—you don't need it—and see whether you can translate the pelvis right and left without rotating it. Some people don't know what they do. As I now look to my right, I see someone who stands on the knee to the right very well, but can not stand on the left knee. Therefore the movement of the pelvis to the right is extensive and to the left restricted. You'll see of course it's the hip joint; the abductors and adductors of the hip joint are very different on one side than the other. Therefore the whole structure including the shoulders must be different.

Now, don't bend your feet; just shift the weight from one knee to the other without lifting anything. You see, by lifting the knee we rotate the pelvis. You do small rotations like this in walking. But if you want to check if one hip joint works as well as the other, then the rotation must be eliminated as much as possible, so that you can attend to whether the sliding of the pelvis to the right and left is as it can be. This means that the synergistic action of the antagonistic muscles, the adductors and the abductors, is the best possible.

For each person, the gait is peculiar, so that anyone can recognize it even 500 yards away. That is because you recognize that one leg and one hip joint moves differently. You can see it in the shoulder and armswing. Then you can say, that's my father, that's my beloved, just from seeing the peculiar way where both sides are not equal. You know then there is a special wobble—a kind of duck walk that is peculiar to my beloved (laughter). Now, make a small movement. You'll find that if you do that gently, your knees will improve. If you don't do it gently, your knees will be very painful.

Now would you please stand on your knees again, and put your right foot on top of your left ankle behind the heel. Join your knees together, and gently, slowly, move your pelvis backwards as if to sit back on the heel which is nearest. Don't sit, but just gradually go back and return. To go a little bit lower comfortably, would you please move the big toes a little apart from one another, and sit back again without strain. Now open your knees very wide; but very wide doesn't mean crazily wide. Do the same thing, and notice that your big toes went apart by themselves a little bit more. Your feet must be crossed, unless you have some trouble that doesn't allow you to do it. Now change over your feet and do the same thing.

Stop the movement. Stand on the knees with your feet still with one over the other, and slide your pelvis right and left until you feel that you stand a little better on one knee. Don't lift your knees, but just move your pelvis so that you feel that you stand on one knee harder, so that if you wanted to lift the other one, you could. Now join your knees again. For some people the difference between opening and joining is barely perceptible. In other words: the difference is so great that it makes the movement impossible. Therefore, see what you can do to make *your* movement more comfortable, and continue to slide your pelvis right and left.

Now lift both feet off the floor, and stand on your toes as if for running. Slowly—you won't be able to stand on both like that, unless your knees are separated. Leave your knees together for now. Then one foot can stand on the toes as if for running and the other one can't.

Now, move back as if to sit. Slowly, because if you're not used to it you'll break your toes and extend the Achilles tendon so that it will be painful. Be extra careful if you have some sensitivity in your knees. We are moving the knees in a non-habitual way. If you have discomfort you'll find that the rest of the lesson won't work well. You can't learn with discomfort, with apprehension, with challenge, with hurrying.

So find a soft pillow to put under your knees if you need it. It must be pleasant to learn. The impossible is made feasible only when it's comfortable, pleasant to do. If it isn't pleasant to do, you will not do it anyway after you learn it; you'll never use it. Without comfort the body will *never* learn, and will refuse to accept it. You'll never learn to put a cigarette into your eye and like it. You'll never learn to sit on a drawing pin when the pin is upwards, and if you *learn* to do that you're so crazy that you deserve it.

Now would you please stand on your knees again. Change

over your feet so that the other foot can stand on the toes and slowly go back. Now open your knees very wide and then both feet will probably be able to stand on the toes. But each person in the group stands differently. Some are more comfortable than others. Change back and forth until you can feel the difference between the way you use your toes of one foot and the other. Those of you that have trouble with your feet have eliminated this movement from use *years* ago. You will see that you can recuperate with this movement much faster than you would ever suspect possible.

To improve further, put both feet apart normally, and then stretch your feet so that you touch the floor with the nails of the toes. Then bend them and flex your feet until you can stand on your toes as if getting up to run. You'll see that if you facilitate by moving your pelvis to and fro, the movement becomes possible. That is, to put your toes flexed the pelvis moves forward, and you can lift your legs as far as is necessary to stand on your toes. Move the pelvis down as if to sit, when your feet are extended and try to put your feet the other way round, then you must move the pelvis. So start by facilitating the movement, and then you'll find that once the tendons of your feet get their normal flexion and extension, you can do the movement without moving your pelvis. But don't do that now. Only the best pupils find it possible. As you know the best pupils with us are the people who interfere with learning. If you try to be the best pupil you will flex them too much and there will be pain and they will never flex or extend properly.

Now would you please sit or lie on the floor and rest. Again stand on your knees. Put your knees in a comfortable way, and now translate or slide your pelvis right and left, and see the difference. Is it getting better, easier, clearer now that you don't tilt your pelvis? When you slide your pelvis, you do something in the back, in the spine: movements that are normally not done. Now see if you can go so much to the right, and so much to the left, and a little bit more, and see what happens. There comes a moment when you feel that one knee must go forward, and the other knee must go backwards. At the beginning the easy thing is to let the knee that has no weight go in the direction which feels right. There is one direction which is a better way for you; find out which knee tends to go forward when you move your pelvis to the right.

Stop; put your right hand into the left; place your hands on the floor, and standing like that put the top of your head just above your forehead into your hands. Rock your pelvis to and fro, forward and backwards. Observe what you feel your shoulders and your spine do. Are you doing that movement with your shoulders, with sinking your spine? You will if your elbows are too wide or too narrow.

Now put your elbows close to one another, and rock forward, as before. Join your knees and continue. Now, think of your stomach; draw it in and push it out; make it go near to the floor. Some don't know how far their knees should be from their elbows, and therefore they can't do it. Another way to do the movement is to imagine that somebody has a foot on the small of your back, you push him up and let him down. As you go forward, you draw your stomach in and your spine rounds itself at a peculiar point. And now roll forward enough to flex your feet and stand on your toes. Do the same movement with your abdomen. Your heels must be close together or touch. You have to do it slowly until your feet can stand on your toes properly. Observe only that you're moving not as far backwards to sit, and the movement of your stomach can be done only if you do something different with your arms and head.

Now stretch your feet, and continue. Stop a minute. [Moshé asks one group member to come forward.] Would you please come here? Stand on your knees again; put your right hand into the left, and organize your head the way you feel comfortable—forehead or top of the head. Now, join the knees, move forward and backwards, and observe your lumbar region. It should go up and down and as easily as you can go without straining. Do a few movements, and then stand on your toes and do a few movements. Then open your knees wide, and keep on doing the same thing. Do you remember the sinking movement of the spine? As you move forward and backwards, your spine gets round, not only in the lumbar region, but also in between the shoulder blades. You'll find that your shoulder blades go apart when you move forward, only if you suddenly use the cervical spine. The vertebrae there pile up on one another in such a way that you could stand on your head without effort. We don't intend this now. So continue to move the cervical spine forward. First the lowest 7th vertebra between the shoulder blades. Draw your abdomen in while you go forward, and then you'll see that you have great difficulty in changing the curvature of the cervical spine. That means between the bottom of your skull and that seventh big vertebra that you already use with awareness, the others remain as they are. Don't change them, but note that you have preselected points in the spine that are mobile, but the whole spine is not. That is, a few points are flexible, and the rest is just like a piece of wood. Now we are going to do something about that. Would you please make a point now when you go forward to *lower* your abdomen; doing the inverse of what you did a minute ago.

[Moshé returns to the whole group.] When you go forward, make your stomach pregnant, and observe. Don't press hard. It's not a question of forcing the vertebra to do anything. That's not learning. We must find a way where the vertebra will move. Then the muscles can move properly. Now move your abdomen down to the floor, while you go forward. You must go slowly before you ruin yourselves. Your pelvis must do something different from before while rolling forward. Your pelvis moves the anus *up*. And you can see that some people cannot move the anus up sufficiently to make intercourse in that position comfortable.

Now stretch your feet and continue. Note only whether it's easier to put your head on your hands at a different point. You'll find that you feel that you want to go higher on your head. Go forward and draw your stomach in, and *stay* there and push your stomach out. Observe what happens in your neck, and observe what your shoulder blades do to your spine, whether you think of it or not. Actually you're thinking; otherwise nothing would happen.

Now stop. Lie on your back, and rest a little. There's a very peculiar feeling now, in your spine, neck, head, and in the trunk, a feeling of getting taller. It is not just a feeling; you are actually taller. That is because some unnecessary curvatures in the spine are reduced to what they are in a young child or in a more perfectly organized human being. If you listen to yourself, you'll note that the neck between your head and back is different. If you try to roll your head right and left, you'll be surprised. For those who hear it creaking, there is a range where there's no creaking any more. The movement is very, very fine in the middle, and on the larger angle from the middle to the right and to the left, though it is rarely equal on both sides.

Roll to the side and again stand on your knees. Put your left hand into the right, and place your head in your hands a little bit higher than your forehead. This time open your knees a little bit, lift your right knee off the floor, and slowly put it behind your left knee on the floor. Stretch your feet completely so that the nails touch the floor. Now very, very gently rock your body forward and backwards, drawing your stomach in when you go forward, and letting it out when you go backwards. But observe: your pelvis does something that you do not intend. Now move forward and press the abdomen down. As you do this, you expand and flatten your chest. Now go forward with your abdomen down and find out which elbow is feasible to lift, and which one is much harder to lift.

Now, find out whether you can now move the free shoulder blade together with the other. As you lift the free shoulder, what does your pelvis do? Do you notice that you stand on the knee differently than before? Now move your right shoulder blade only—towards the middle—and lift your right elbow. Note what the rest of your body does, and how you stand on your knee. Your right hip joint is capable of going forward and backward, and allows your knees to stand on the floor. Do it slowly, and since it's difficult, it's very interesting to make it easy and comfortable. Stop; lie; rest a little bit. Lie on your back if you prefer, just to *see* and to *feel* which parts have worked harder than the others, and in which parts there is a change more marked than in the other. Your body is quite asymmetrical in places where you wouldn't expect it at all.

Now would you please roll on your side, and get up on your knees. Put your left hand into the right, lean on your head as nearly to the top as you feel comfortable. Spread your shoulders and your knees so that when you look in between you could see both feet quite easily, and rock forward and backward. When you rock, feel which vertebrae can come into play now between your lumbar and cervical spine. Then see whether you can, going forward, move the upper part of your spine so forward that you need to move the shoulder blades apart. Therefore go forward quite a lot, and then, at that position, stay, lift your left knee, and place it behind the right knee. If you find that you can't stand on the left knee, stand on the right knee only with the left hanging where it is. The movement that we do afterwards will help organize it.

Now slowly rock forward and backwards and listen to the big cervical vertebra and the lumbar spine. When you rock forward, notice what happens to all the other vertebrae from the back of the skull to the middle of the shoulders. Unless you do something peculiar with yourself nothing happens there. While you do that would you please take your left hand and put it on the floor as if for pushing up. Your head stays in your right hand. Now continue forward and back. And observe whether your left knee begins to stand there. Switch and put your left hand underneath your head, and put your right hand as if for pushing up. Have a look at what happens. Now go forward drawing your stomach in, and when you're forward, stay there and push your stomach out. Note what happens: where does your chin go? Put both hands as for pushing up. Continue rocking forward and backwards, and then push your abdomen out. Don't lift your head off the floor. Now put both feet and knees symmetrically, widen them, and then put your toes as if for running and both hands as if you're pushing up. Continue going forward and backwards, and push your body forward and backwards. Your elbows must be in the air and your hands must be in a place where they could lift your shoulders if you wanted to.

Stop; lie on your back and rest. Stand on your hands and your knees again. Put your left hand on the floor with the back of your hand on the floor. Put your right cheek on the left palm. Stretch your right arm out with the palm to the ceiling to your right. There's only one way of doing it. Now very slowly slide your pelvis as you did before right and left. Go very slow or some necks may suffer. Slide your pelvis right and left, so that you feel you are standing on one knee more than on the other. You gradually move from one knee to the other. Do just the small movement that is easy and comfortable to do.

Stop a minute. This time draw your stomach in and push it out, gently. You'll find that you have to move your pelvis a little bit forward. Find out which parts of the spine didn't bend up to now. You'll see it's not the lumbar spine that we're dealing with now, and not the cervical. The cervical vertebrae do some sort of movement. But in between you'll find a whole lump of vertebrae that have never moved, or nearly never moved, with most people. As you continue you'll find that the pressure on the cheek shifts nearer to the chin on the cheek, and then to the forehead. Push your abdomen in and out. Stretch out on your stomach and rest.

Go back to the same position, but put your left hand as for pushing up and your right palm underneath your right cheek. Where would you put your right elbow? Put it *first* near to you in between your legs, put the hand on that, and continue the movement, pushing your abdomen up and down. Use your left hand to help you. Your toes and feet are stretched. Move your right elbow out to your right, pivoting on the palm of your hand, and *not in one go*. [Moshé interrupted to comment on a group member.] I can't understand it; it's such an awkward position. He actually lifts himself and moves in a big bang. Therefore he has done a useless movement, unnecessary for what we do. Go back again between your legs, and move it gradually by 1/10 of a degree. Organize yourself and breathe shallowly. You use the weight in the legs in such a way that you can move your elbow a little bit to the right, and a little bit to the left. Go slow until you can feel you can do it. You're not obliged to succeed immediately, you're not at school— you're learning. When you have learned, you'll see the amount of speed and power with which you'll be able to do the same thing.

Now, put both hands underneath your right cheek. Your elbows must be placed somewhere reasonable. You can't put them wherever you want. There are places which are best for you. Observe: is your right elbow now further away from your knees than the left? Is your chin touching your left shoulder, or not? Now move your elbows apart as wide as you can. And now lift your left knee, and move it behind the right knee to the right. Move slowly; don't break your neck. Don't use your toes and don't change the position of your knees after you move.

Any movement that is learned in such a way that you have to do a preliminary re-arrangement in order to execute it, means that your system is badly organized. So slowly shift your weight onto the right knee and so that the left knee can go gently and smoothly behind, and can be taken out as smoothly and as easily. Stay there and move your pelvis right and left. Notice how the pressure on your cheek varies. Move your pelvis right and left, then slowly forward and backwards.

Now very slowly bring your legs to stand equally on both knees. This time put your left hand as for pushing up, and move your right hand on the floor to carry your head towards your left hand, and back. Do it without lifting; just reduce the pressure, so your hand can slide. Now move your head under into that gate formed by your left elbow slowly, circularly. Move your right hand with your head and elbow circularly forward. Then move your nose and fingers under that gate. It's very difficult, you can do only a small movement. If anybody wants to do a big movement, he can kill himself if he wants.

Now move your right elbow, nearer to you and away from

you as far as you can, carrying your head and right cheek on your hand. Slowly stretch out your right arm to the right, with the palm upwards. Go to the extreme right, now move your head underneath the gate. You need a lot of skill in your hips and legs. So don't succeed in one movement. You need to distribute your effort equally all along your body. You hold the breath; it's crazy. This lesson is supposed to teach you to make difficult things easy and comfortable, beyond any expectation. It's not a question of succeeding in the movement; we can take any other movement to learn that.

Now, slowly move your head and stand on the toes of your left foot. While you go forward see where you could lift your left knee a little bit off the floor, but your foot stays on the floor. There is such a strain on the spine, that if you do that fast, you only do harm to yourself. Your head goes under the gate and your left knee lifts gently off the floor. Your right arm must be stretched to the right with the palm upwards. Some people are so involved that unless somebody bangs them on the head they don't hear that I repeat myself ten times. Continue and lift your left knee a tiny bit. Let your left hand support your body. Your left elbow must be in the air, and your hand presses *somewhere* where it can take away part of the pressure on your head. We do it this way so your head and spine have the leisure to move.

Stop. Slowly sit up in any way which is comfortable, but provided there is some sort of symmetry in your pelvis. Slowly turn your head to the right, and then look to the left. Notice the difference. To the right is the way you have always turned until today. Now turn to the left. See how you *really are.* This is the side from which we took away the *residual* junk that we carry with ourselves *uselessly.* The difference is that your head, pelvis, and shoulder have learned. And don't try to re-establish the symmetry! Because thereby you'll lose the learning. If you go right and left, you'll have the same result as all your gymnastics.

I want you to make a trial to find out that there's a difference. If you exercise you avoid the ability of absorbing it in your system, as we said about taking in food. You *have* to *assimilate*. Therefore your brain assimilates information from the right hemisphere to the left. What we have done now we have done with the right hemisphere, and therefore what will pass from one to the other you won't be able to lose or forget until you're dead. It will be *easily* recoverable.

Please get up, and observe what you feel like. Turn to your right round yourself and turn to the left. The whole lesson was done without symmetry. Can you feel the difference turning to the right and turning to the left? There's such a difference that everyone can feel it. Now stand one minute, and make one movement to the right with your head, eyes, and the same to the left. Make it simple. There's a tremendous difference in rotation between one and the other. In other words, the normal way of looking to the right is a small part of what you can do normally, effortlessly. Anyway, thank you very much. (applause)

LESSON TEN:
JAW, TONGUE AND AGGRESSION

Sit in any position comfortable for you. Put your tongue to the right side of your inner jaw. You can open the mouth, or not as you wish. Now *count* with the tip of your tongue from the wisdom teeth to the middle of your mouth. How many pairs of teeth can you count? Move the tip of your tongue, touch the two or three top ones, and lower ones and identify them, and then move to the other pair and see how many pairs have you got. Allow yourself to breathe as you continue. At the beginning you find that you count rapidly. But in fact you don't know how many there are. You do not feel them clearly. Go over to the left from the middle to the wisdom teeth, and count. How do you count? Everybody can count, but how is it done? To what do we direct our attention when we count? It's not so simple to answer. Now go from the left to the right, and see whether you didn't count wrongly. Watch, do you really have to press your tongue so hard? It's only counting; it should be a mental exercise.

Now has anyone thought what we do when we count? Lie down a minute, and see whether you can count the fingers of your right hand. But really count them, as if you didn't know how many there are. We don't even have to look when we count. But now count the toes on the left foot, and see which toes can you count and which toes you just *know* by your previous experience. But count them, and find out whether it's different from counting in the hand. It shouldn't be different.

Yet, count the middle toe. Can you feel the middle toe? If you can't feel it, you can't count it.

Now look at the fireplace. Count how many stones are there on the arc. How do you do that? Somebody else can count the panels; count them and see what you do in order to count. Now count mentally from 1 to 7 and see what you do to count. But actually imagine that there're seven people, seven men, seven oranges, seven anything. How do we manage to do it? By doing what? Now, lie on your side and count how many vertebra there are from the cervical 7th big vertebra to the free-floating ribs, but not with your hands. Why can't you count them? You count on your hand? Now count these vertebrae by touching each one, and see whether you can do that. Very difficult; you can't reach them very well, and you have to manipulate all sorts of things. Now think of that! How does it come about that you can count the fingers of your hand, or your toes or the stones there, but you can't count your own vertebrae? Obviously we're doing something which makes the difference. Why is it difficult to find where the third toe is on your foot? Why is it easy to find the small one? If I ask you to count the toes, if you're really honest, you find that you can't count them. You can count from the left side. There's the small toe, the big toe, the second toe, but the third one, it is *very* difficult to perceive and to know where it is. Obviously you have to do something to count it.

Can you count from 37 to 31 backwards? What are you doing? What are you counting? There is nothing there, there's only something you think about. And count how many figures do you see from 37 to 31. And if you count them inclusively, they're not what the subtraction would make it. Therefore in counting them you'll find another figure, and it's not 6 but 7 numbers. As you count backwards, you *say,* 37. What do you do to find the next one? We think, but doing *what?* How do you know that's the second number backwards? To *what* do you draw your attention in order to be able to count? Suppose you take 37 and then you count how many numbers there are if you go down to 36 and then up to 38, 37 is neutral. Now, you go to 39 and back to 35, up to 40. How many numbers have you counted?

By doing operations like that, it may dawn on you what we're doing. What we actually count are the number of shifts of attention; whatever we do, whatever it is, your fingers, your eyes, your hands, we count the number of shifts of attention. Now we can learn to do something else. Listen to that. Everybody knows that that's 1 (knocking on something) that's 2. (2 taps) How many am I doing now?

[Moshé taps rapidly.]

If I make very quick taps and you can't shift your attention you don't know—you can't count (dialogue). It's a very funny thing too, if you try to do 21 taps, and go fast, you can't count them yourself. (tapping) You couldn't know whether you were correct. But then make marks by tapping on a piece of paper and close your eyes. Say to yourself, eleven, and you'll be astonished to find when you finish that it's eleven. If you took a large number like twenty-seven, which seems impossible, and repeat ten times, you'll find that the number of times you're correct is out of proportion to the probability to get any of the numbers between one and 27. If you train yourself like that, you will be able to mark any number of dots you choose without counting, and without paying any attention, and be astonished to find counting the dots afterwards that the dots are the number you wanted.

Now close your eyes and count how many windows there really are in your home. Notice that you shift your attention from one window to the other and count the shifts. And if you don't put them in a given order according to the rooms, you'll miss one, like the other window in the kitchen, or the other window in the bathroom. Now how many panes are there? Usually not the same number as the number of windows. Again you actually count the number of shifts of attention.

Therefore counting is a subjective sort of business. If you don't count the number of shifts of your eyes, or ears, or tongue, you can't count.

Now put your tongue between your teeth, and count the

upper teeth touching them from the outside from the left wisdom tooth. As you continue counting each one easily, gently, you will find that it's a question of attention. Your tongue needn't make big efforts, but just enough to realize that there is another tooth to perceive. Now go from right to left. You could do it with your fingers of course, but you'll find that using your tongue has another merit. Move your tongue again, around your upper jaw from the outside between your jaw and teeth. You may open your mouth, or not. Note only that when you count, you actually count the shifts of attention, nothing else. Therefore the number of teeth you will find will depend on the number of teeth you attend to—one after the other. If two teeth have no separation, like a bridge which is smooth, and there is no shift of attention—i.e., you feel the same sensation—you cannot tell whether that bridge takes the place of 3 or 2 or 4 teeth. We learned to count when we were young children. We never realized that we counted each shift of attention.

Now that you know that, stop for a moment and see whether you can actually locate the middle toe on your left foot. Now count from your middle toe, one toe to the right, one toe to the left. Can you see how wooly that is? We can not shift our attention to something that is outside our ability to feel. Now would you please sit, and touch the middle toe, and count one toe to the right and one to the left. Note the clarity of that compared with the wooliness of shifting attention to something which you don't perceive clearly.

Here is an example! Someone plays a very simple tune on the piano. We ask him: how many times did he hit the keys with his fingers? If he played a quarter of a minute, not many, but he would find it practically impossible to count. On the other hand if he knew that he were to count, he would realize that it's possible to do. Now he would clearly pay attention to the number of different notes, i.e., the number of shifts of attention. Try it yourself. You can play it first without being able to tell how many notes. Then play the same tune. After 3 trials you can count the notes, because you realized what you're doing. If you can't, it seems miraculous if somebody does. But some people find the way to do it on their own. Counting is the origin of arithmetic. Before arithmetic was taught in the school, our ancestors needed to feel that they could count.

When we examine different cultures and different peoples, we find that they count in a different way and shift their attention differently. Those of you who can play the piano, try to play in your imagination; you will see the clarity with which you can perceive because you have shifts of attention in your hand and ear. Imagine both, and they corroborate each other—it becomes clear, definite, unmistakable.

There are many curious things about shifts of attention. Take your left index finger, and grasp it between the index and middle fingers of your right hand. When you touch your fingers like that, you'll find there is one index finger of your left hand. It is so unmistakable that there is no question. Since you touch your left index finger with both the index and the middle finger, your right hand should have two sensations and you would think you would count two not one. Well, why don't you shift your attention from the right index to the right middle finger?

Let's find out. Cross your middle finger over your index finger on your right hand. Now grasp your left index finger with your right fingers as crossed. As you are used to count two sensations for one, move your crossed fingers around and you will find that you have two index fingers to your sensation. Now you *do* count your shifts of attention. But you are so used to take two for one, that you don't question what you do. You shift your attention from what you *feel* to what you know. You will find now that if you shift your attention from your left index finger to the two surrounding fingers of your right hand, you can feel clearly that it touched two fingers. So it's clear that the right hand feels one finger with two fingers and the left feels two fingers with one. But notice that it is difficult to relinquish what you know and actually take your perception, your feeling as the correct information.

You can see that for most people feelings are not reliable information; it depends on the habit. Therefore, you may feel in love, but it is not true love. When you actually taste something, you find you don't love it. And the other way around— You think you dislike a person; then you suddenly find, on making contact, that you like that person better than anyone else you know.

Touch your fingers again. It will take you quite a while before the two fingers to your sensation will feel as one. Continue until you feel one finger between your index and middle fingers. Now you will be suprised and you will shift to the normal—You will feel two. But for that you will have to persist for a few minutes until the *feeling* is so clear that you don't try to think and measure and consider whether you are doing it right or wrong. Now you can feel it both ways. Before we had *learned* to consider the two shifts of attention as one. We did that by agreement.

Most of what is socially common to everyone is really an agreement, not a physiological fact. Physiologically you would find that if you cross fingers as you did, you can find *three* index fingers, provided you touch at uncommon places that are not used to touching together. This is how young children, when learning in school, make mistakes. They have learned one and two are three but when you ask them, they don't know. At the beginning of school learning, children have to learn to abstract and answer, not in terms of what they feel, but what is required. And so they learn the feeling of two index fingers with the fingers around the index finger like that, *means* one finger. If you watch children with this understanding, you will understand how they make errors.

Most of us imitate the usual trend of the culture and give up our individuality to a degree that necessitates that in every generation, of a hundred thousand people you need at least a thousand psychiatrists to make life possible. As a result we have hundreds of systems and a crop of techniques to develop your sensory awareness and develop your feeling. That there are so many shows you that none of them know really what the problem is and haven't got the methods of solving it. Otherwise, there would be a science of awareness as there's only *one* science of physics. There's only one science of biology, physiology, architecture. For the things that we know truly, we don't have fifteen systems. The systems merge together and though there are different opinions, different schools, none of them hate each other. Just consider the business of diets. How many diets do you know? Obviously that shows you that we actually are so alienated from our feelings that anybody who gives us guidance and is right in 10% of what he says, we find, 'Oh look, that's better than my own credo.'

I did not think of that before, because I couldn't rely on my feeling before; I never dared to. When I did dare, I was told, 'You're dreaming—you're not here. Pay attention. You're at school. Don't dream.' And in class when you wanted to rely on your feelings for a *second,* the teacher didn't allow you that. You were instructed, 'Don't look out the window, don't look at the birds there. Don't look through the window, look to the board. Or to the book—or to the copybook.'

Now, please find out whether you can open your mouth and put the lower teeth touching the top ones. You will observe, when you do that, you make faces as ugly as we really are. Try again and see that it is not so terrible. You move the *jaw* and don't just open your mouth. You will see that the way we hold our lips and form our mouth is a result of the fact that we never make that movement at all. Most jaws are actually not doing the full movement. And that is related to why most voices are inferior in quality and in power to what they are when you take a few lessons with a good teacher.

Now, put the lower teeth in again and take them out. Note that your jaw is so articulated that when you open your mouth your head need not move at all. But you will find that many people will lift their head to open their mouth.

If you want to open it, to open it *really,* then you will see that you move your head back—except good singers.

Actually to open your mouth your jaw should make a circular movement. From here you should open it, *as if* the lower teeth were in front of the upper teeth.

Take your jaw again, with your lower teeth in front of the

upper teeth, and open your mouth. Now your mouth opens much larger than usual. Do it again and you will observe that the musculature is so arranged about the neck and jaw that in opening wide, most people take the head back. So let us examine: is your jaw part of your head or face? Well, one of the sockets is part of the head and the jaw itself is part of the face, depending on which you call face and which you call head. You see, if you find the head of a skeleton without the jaw, you say you found a head—you don't say you didn't find a head. (laughter) You don't say you found a face but the jaw is not there—or *is* there; it's still a skull, you see.

Would you please continue that movement at least a dozen times; take the lower teeth forward with your mouth open and then closed. You will find that you improve so much that your normal bite changes from touching on only one tooth or two to the lot touching. We wouldn't deform our jaw, if we didn't prohibit children from doing such a movement from the start.

Now do it with your mouth open and a few times with your mouth closed. When it is clear, open your jaw, and move your jaw to the right and left. Don't move your mouth, just the jaw. And note whether you do it the same to the right and to the left. For some, you do it smoothly to the right, but to the left you do it like coming to a wall. Obviously it's not the same. Watch, if you want to see whether you do it equally; one side is smooth and easy and you can stop before the end, and then to the other side you go to the limit and go against a soft wall.

Make an accent on one side and not on the other. Now, if you feel you remove the accent from this side, then move with an accent on the other side. Continue until you feel you make no accent here or there and move on both sides equally.

All right now, stop for a minute and then move your tongue right and left touching the inside of the upper teeth and the lower teeth as you did at the beginning. Now move your tongue without touching your teeth. What does it feel like to move the tongue alone?

Would you please pay attention: open your mouth from where it is now and stop. Put the lower teeth in front of the upper teeth and open again and you'll find that you open the mouth about twice as wide as before. Your mouth should open normally so that you can put two fingers between your teeth. If you just open without putting your jaw forward, the fingers won't fit. The problem is that one should be able to open the mouth. Once you take the lower teeth in front of the upper teeth there is no problem.

A singer must open the mouth to make the sound of AW (Note: phonetically like *saw*). If you watch a trained singer like Callas, then you will see that she could not sing as she does without opening her mouth *so* large that most people would think that it's artifically done. Some like Fisher-Dieskan actually think of opening their mouth, and you will see that the mouth opens by itself an incredible amount when they say AW.

There are many funny things about such sounds. How do the people begin to know to write vowels, consonants? In the ancient languages such as Hebrew you write the letters and you have special signs which can be put on each letter which will connect the consonant with any vowel you want. For instance, watch my mouth and you will see how it is done. If you write a B and put a dot underneath it's $B\overline{E}$ and therefore it will be eeeeeee (long sound). Just a hole in the mouth. B-eeeeee. Watch what I do with my mouth to pronounce eeeee ——the lips don't move. . . . only in the middle a little . . . eeeee. And that *dot* is eee, which is the form of the mouth to make the sound eeee. You can put the dot under B, it is bee; a dot under L is lee, and a dot under D is dee.

Now the symbol, ־, under the consonant gives the formation of the lips for the vowel sound AH-HHHHH. Say AH-HHHHH (note: as in mamma). You must open the mouth and teeth. A pass like ־ is AH; when you put that under b it's bah, you put it under an l, it's lah, and under k it's kah. Children learn that —and when they can learn the diphthong they don't need it; they can write only the consonants. You say 'bridge,' but write brd and that's finished. Therefore any book translated from *any* language into Hebrew is 70% shorter because all the vowels are thrown away. *No one* doubts a country without vowels.

Now you will see that all the vowels represent the aperture of the mouth. For instance, three dots is 'EH', beh, leh, keh, meh. Now 'O' is the dot on top; and that is $\overline{O}$-OOOOO. If you photograph the mouths of a dozen people and note the particular formation of their mouth to pronounce that vowel, you will see that all the Hebrew vowels with the dots represent the form of the mouth, and the movement that we make with the mouth in order to pronounce that vowel.

Now, would you please curve your mouth again and put your lower teeth to the front and on top of the upper teeth. Open your lips. How do you open your lips? There are two ways of doing it; which one do you use? Now do the other one. . . . and the other one, and gradually reduce the intensity. Look, most of you do it like that. . . . (laughter) . . . with a hardly aggressive movement. You know why? Because we inhibit aggression in children, which is idiotic. It's incorrect. It's because people don't distinguish between aggression and violence. But aggression is an essential part of life. Biting an apple is aggression. You break the apple, bite it, and tear off a piece of flesh; it's what a leopard does when he devours a living thing and the same as when dogs tear a piece of flesh out of someone. So aggression is essential; we couldn't live without it. But there's a great difference between aggression and violence. If you eat an apple violently, you will see the difference between aggression and violence. You could eat an apple with such absolute violence that you would disgust anybody (laughter). People are afraid of violence. That's why when you put your teeth forward, people see an ugly, frightened face. Try for yourself Put the lower teeth ahead of the top and then open your lips wide. Then you will see that in most faces it is a face of fear and violence. Thus we have eliminated that movement from our repertoire. And if you want to make somebody open his mouth for a photograph and smile you ask him to say cheese. Then the mouth is not violent. Now make the movement of a smile about a dozen times, with your lips joined and then open.

Observe your intensity. Couldn't you make it soft? With your hand you could move your lips easily. Do it with your hand and notice.

It's a curious thing, for the mouth is the part with which we begin to know the outside world. Since we use our mouth first, all the sensations of the mouth are very precise. The tongue is very delicate and the lips have one of the best innervations with very close, very fine fibers. These are more delicate than in the hand and the tips of the fingers. Yet education is such that we lose part of the ability. Actually, we never learn to differentiate the mouth properly.

Now, observe what happens. Open your jaw and mouth like that. Now soften your mouth and jaw and face. Now find that if you soften and make your mouth wide and open your jaw, you make a smile. If you don't open your mouth, you express aggression or fear of aggression. Gradually you can get to do what you want.

Notice the effect this movement has on people's faces. [Moshé asks people to observe one person.] Her face has been changing since she started. Can you see her mouth . . . how she laughs now? Her face has become more agreeable, more friendly. Because she has eliminated some of the inhibitions that she had since early childhood. All the treatment and diagnosis and analysis and whatever gestalt therapy that you get, didn't reach that. In gestalt . . . you know what you get? .. . . You get ah-hhhhh (crying sounds), and they consider that a treatment. (laughter) *Cry* a little bit. Yes, I prefer you laughing to crying.

You know Charles Darwin, in addition to his other work, had a hobby. This hobby was his exploration of the emotions in animals and in man. One key question he studied was whether laughter is a learned behavior, a part of culture or whether it is a biological movement. Thus he sought out isolated places in the world where communication with other cultures was unlikely or very improbable, and where there was a population different from others in habits, taboos, and normal behavior, as well as language. In these places he wanted to find out if people laugh and cry as we do. For he questioned whether these behaviors were a biological or physiological necessity or a thing that we learn from the mother.

It's not so simple a question. For example if I shake my head right and left, do I mean yes or no? Well you might think that is a natural movement. It isn't. Because the Turks do the exact opposite. The movement we use for approval they use for negation with an accent upwards. Bedouins and Arabs, in order to say, 'Come here,' don't gesture as we do. To them, 'come here' is this——'Tal, tal.' When they sit in a doorway and you see them make that gesture, it looks like they want you to go away. So they say, 'Tal, Tal!,' meaning, 'come here.' And if he wants you to go away look what he does, (Arab words) 'Yalar..ch.' So it is different from what we do.

So Darwin had a problem in finding out whether laughing is a physiological action or a cultural habit. But here is how he investigated the question. First he noted an extraordinary thing. He found that many animals open the mouth to show violence and snarl. [Moshé demonstrates and snarls.] Of course, the mouth opens sufficiently to bite. So you put the jaw forward, . . . (snarling sounds) . . . (laughter) . . . but that is what our ancestors did when they hunted. Then he examined anatomically which muscles are involved in laughter. He observed how one used the muscles of eyes, the nostrils (Moshé snarls again) and other high muscles of the face. He listed each muscle used and made some approximate measure of how much they contract in order to produce laughter, or a smile.

Using photographs and drawings he noted that the movements to produce laughter or smiling were the same in any culture. Even with cultures that had no contact with any others, this was true. And so he concluded that laughing and smiling were biological-physiological acts.

When Darwin returned to England after his travels he made a further observation that struck him as so important he wrote about it afterwards. At the zoo he watched children feed peanuts to the gorillas, chimpanzees, orangutans. Everything was all right. But when the children began to laugh, the orangutans moved away, showed their teeth and became aggressive. Snarling, they beat their cages with their hands. It dawned on him that the aggressive expression of showing the teeth with a snarl was, if you reduce the intensity, the same as a smile. [Moshé demonstrates (snarl)]..and then it's a smile. Laughter is realizing that the danger is to somebody else, not to you.

I don't know whether you have read Darwin's book on the expression of emotion, but he showed that the animals, which are not long out of the jungle, have not yet lost their ancestral instinctive or reflective responses. Thus when an animal sees the teeth bared he will respond to that with anything but gentleness. Therefore the chimps and gorillas were alright when they were given peanuts. But when the children laughed at the way they ate them (eating sounds), they bared their teeth in laughing. The animal took that for aggression. For most people, when they laugh, you can see that the face actually expresses anger, aggression, violence.

Now, would you please now denude both the upper and the lower teeth? And look at her face. Can you see? It's aggressive. Now soften and relax to a smile. Now continue baring the teeth and softening. Open your jaws until you can make a soft, controllable movement which fits your present character and not the violence that you have never really mastered. Now imagine yourself *really* angry with someone. Someone you feel comfortable with. Imagine what you would say and how you would express your anger with your mouth. How would you speak? [Moshé begins softly] 'Look, can't you see it would be better, if you wouldn't . . . (transition to shouting) 'Didn't I tell you? Is it the first time I'm telling you that? How could I live with you for so long!' (laughter) You will see that you bare the teeth.

Now slowly make the movement so that it is within your control. Go as wide as you want and as soft. Think of smiling instead of just making the effort. *Make* the effort and realize what you do and stop. This way you'll change violence into aggression. And aggression is essential to life. Without cutting trees we couldn't have toilet paper; without aggression against the outside world we couldn't live. Without deflowering the women you wouldn't be here. That's violence if you want. You can do it violently, you can do it only aggressively, you can do it kindly and gently. Breaking, cutting, joining, deflowering, penetrating; they are essential. Therefore we should be able to differentiate in our movements between violence and aggression.

Would you please now try to pronounce any word to yourself and count to make it easy? You will listen to your own voice. (voices murmuring) By the way, listen to the sound in the room and you will hear that it sounds like people praying in a church. Doesn't it? (laughter) Therefore you can see that we have produced the sort of mood where you can tell aggression from violence. Now if I pray like this: [Moshé shouts in a querulous voice] 'Oh God, I love you. Give me my daily bread! Give me my daily bread! How will you give me my daily bread?' (laughter) Is that prayer? But if I say, (murmuring softly) 'Give us our daily bread,' etc., the voice is soft, without all the strident, disagreeable noises. Now, look at your faces . . . look at her face; can you see how open it is? How frank it is? And you can get a friendly response, a love response, from her more easily than at any other time in her life. (laughter)

Would you please make sure that your voice is half an octave or an octave lower than usual. Talk to yourself and listen. (talking) That sounds like prayer. (talking) Now take your usual mask and present yourself in the way you speak outside. (talking and laughter) How do you speak to the teacher who examines you, or the policeman who gives you a ticket? (laughter)

Now stop and think, or don't think. You can sleep and do nothing if you want. Just see if you can fix in your attention: how do we count? What do we actually do to count? Can you remember the third toe of your foot? And how many feet did you find that you have? And in this position would you please open your mouth and put the lower teeth on the top ones and move your chin right and left with the mouth like that. See whether you can remove any superfluous tension in your jaw to move it right and left. Put it in its place, and put it outside with a very smooth, easy, graceful movement. And now watch: open your mouth wide, and hard, and see whether you push your head back.

Try again; put your lower teeth in front of your upper teeth, open your mouth and see how you do it now. Go as wide as you can. You feel that you move your head, almost without exception. Now do the same movement starting with the lower teeth on the upper teeth. You will open, but without violence. Note the difference.

Now relax and observe. What are the things we've done that did not agree with you, or which were unpleasant to you? What seemed far-fetched? Or not very interesting? What was the most interesting thing for you? What was the idea for which you said, 'Oh, that is true. I never thought of that at all'? Was it the distinction between agression and violence? Or was it the movement of the jaw and mouth that not only expresses aggression but also violence? Or was it the mouth form and the relation to the vowels of ancient languages? Or was it the feeling that with the fingers crossed over so that you feel two? Do you remember the whole complication of that? If you continue for some time, when you change to the old position, you again find it two instead of one.

For each of these ideas you could say to someone, 'Look, we passed an afternoon and we heard so many funny, idiotic, and interesting things and we experienced them.' But what is the most interesting thing you would tell them? And what is the first idea that would come to your mind? Remember too to try later to see if you can mark a paper with the number of strokes you wish.

Can you remember things that I didn't mention just now? For example, Darwin, peanuts and orangutans, islands, no connection with culture, smiling, laughing, opening and showing the teeth and the relation to aggression. Look into those ideas you remember, that you recall with interest or wish to tell others about. Perhaps you want to read *The Expression of the Emotions* in *Man and Animals.* Or you may wish to explore some of my thinking in *Body and Mature Behavior* which fits with the way we have been in this lesson.

Now, how do you feel as you lie there? You should realize that the lesson was as hard for me as for any of you in this heat. I saved you from having to move a lot. So, see what a fatherly attitude I have towards you. (laughter)

All right now, get up and see what it feels like when you're standing.

Look at each other's faces and see what your faces express. Which of them express annoyance, aggression, violence? (laughter, talking)

LESSON ELEVEN:
ROCKING THE PELVIS

Please lie on your back. Bend your knees. Put them comfortably on the floor. First place your right hand on your abdomen between your chest and your navel and a little below, so that you can feel your navel. Place your other hand on the sternum, a little nearer to the top of your chest.

And now, draw in your abdomen and expand your chest. Not violently, just aggressively. Change over, push the abdomen out and flatten your chest. Continue doing these motions until they're simple and practically insignificant, so there's no hardness, nor harshness in your movement. Note what happens with your breath as you continue. At what moment do you feel that you breathe in? If you don't think of *how* or *when,* as you move, when does the air come in? Is it when the abdomen is is full, or when the chest is blown up? We can intentionally do both. At the moment, just observe. Is it too powerful, or too sudden, or too well done? Do it badly.

Now, gradually make the movement so fast that you make a very small movement. Go as fast as you can. Do you breathe? Go faster, but don't hurry. [Moshé directs his attention to one group member.] Don't help with your hands. Your right hand is helping your abdomen. Usually when I say, don't help with your right hand, everybody else has stopped helping with the right hand except the person I intended to speak to. You know why she uses her hand? Because she doesn't *feel* what she does. So how could she stop? If you don't know what you are doing, how could you change? How could you do what you want?

Note that you can continue the movement at its own rate and your breathing can go on at its own rate. It doesn't matter how fast you move. Therefore, what do we use to breathe? The diaphragm? The chest? We can go on breathing, and move the chest and abdomen in any rhythm we like, provided we can actually divorce the one movement from the other. I ask again, what is breathing given that you continue alternating the volume of the abdomen and of the chest independently of your breath? So there must be another mechanism for breathing, otherwise your breathing rhythm would have changed to whatever rhythm you picked for the chest-diaphragm movement.

Now breathe in and hold your breath and continue the movement alternating chest and belly. So breathing has nothing to do with the movement of your chest and abdomen. In other words, all the loony stories that they tell you when they teach you singing obviously are wrong.

Now keep on breathing out gently, inaudibly, through your mouth, and continue doing this alternating motion of the chest and belly. But change over your hands, just for the sake of variety. As you continue see now whether you can breathe out separately from the motion of the abdomen and the chest.

Can you see—you can complicate your life—the things you know. When you begin to examine what you think you know, you find that you don't know. And as you don't know, you can hardly do what you want. So most people need breathing exercises, and want breathing exercises. Now stop and lie still; see how your breathing is taking place now.

Put your feet on the floor again with your knees comfortably bent. Turn your toes in. [to one group member] You can't because yours are so turned in that you can't turn in any further. That's why I asked you to turn them in. So turn the feet in so that you look like a pigeon-toed person. Now Charlie Chaplin couldn't do that. Now put your feet like Charlie Chaplin. Many of you don't remember how Charlie Chaplin used to put his feet. And now, between the two extremes find where you are comfortable. If you put your feet to the extreme in order to get Charlie's fame and love and fortune, it's a very good thing, but if you walk like that in the street yourself, you're a miserable human being.

Now would you put your feet in a position normal for you. Lift your heels off the floor and put them back. And lift the forefoot. As you continue also switch from the Charlie Chaplin position and to the toes turned inward position. Now stop; that's how the feet should be, more or less. But I have not spoken correctly. I didn't show you how much. I meant 'should,' in the sense of your own present knowing what you're doing. When you're a little bit better, you will change.

Now, with your knees standing as they are, push your feet on the floor as if you want to push away whatever they stand on. You'll find that your pelvis will push your spine through your chest. You must use the exact pressure with your feet, as if you wanted to move the thing on which they stand away from you. Make a small gentle movement; push and let go. Observe what do you feel in your pelvis as you do that? Keep on rocking continuously. But don't lift the pelvis off the floor.

Now, move your feet another foot away from your buttocks. And rock. Is that comfortable? Some people find that's the best way of rocking. But this is much too far away. Now, put the feet as close as you can. Lift your pelvis and get your heels as close to the buttocks as you can. Now rock your pelvis. Between those idiotic limits find the one that fits you. And now rock and you will see that it's really better.

The pelvis rocks in a funny way and the femurs press in the socket of the joint to push the pelvis. When we walk, we also push with our legs. So what position should your pelvis take? Many say there are correct positions: inclined forward, inclined backward. But are they speaking about the upper part or the lower part? In most books they say to bend the pelvis forward; if you bend the upper part forward the lower part goes backward. What sort of movement do you want? 'Straighten your pelvis,' meaning straightening what? The lower part or the upper part? It's a tremendous difference. Then I say, 'Move the pelvis forward.' Which is the pelvis? The upper part? The lower part? Or the middle? The middle is moving neither forward or backward, so . . . it's as clear as mud.

Now, would you please see that when you push with the legs to rock, in order to repeat again you let go. Now when you let go, you can also *pull* the floor with your legs so that you make the largest movement possible with your pelvis. Try now to push the floor with your feet and pull with your feet and find out what happens to your feet and to your pelvis. Don't use power. Tell me, in which direction are the knees drawn together and in which are the knees moved apart? When you push upwards, the more the push is in the direction of the movement of the spine the more efficient it is. Your nervous system will do everything it can to draw your knees together to do it. That is, pressure on your legs downward will bring the hip joint to as effective a position as possible. The biggest effect will occur when the plane of the leg is parallel to the spine, and you will have the most effective push.

Now, this time continue rocking but make it so that it is not discrete, but oscillatory. It should be continuous and repetitive at a certain rhythm. You allow your body to return to its position by itself and therefore the push becomes jelly-like. Do you know what *p'chah* is? What is it in English? If you take the tendinous parts of the legs of a pork or a cow and boil them, you produce a jelly when you let it cool. If you move that jelly, it vibrates approximately as your pelvis does now. Continue and note what happens to your spine and head. When you push your pelvis up, the upper part goes back and the lower part, the coccyx, goes away from the floor while the back of the lumbar spine is pressed to the floor. The upper part of the pelvis moves backwards. Continue and note whether you can feel that the spine goes through the chest like a skewer through meat. Because the weight of your chest, and pelvis is great enough, and friction is present, you can pull only as far as the skin, tissues, and muscles of the back can move. And your chest and pelvis can rock to adjust to that push. Try and you will see. If you keep on rocking, you will feel that actually your pelvis, lumbar spine and chest will organize themselves in such a way that they really lie on the floor together. Moving upwards your chin goes away from your chest and downwards your chin goes near to your chest. If it doesn't you hold your breath, and have involuntary, unconscious stiffening somewhere. The sooner you feel that, the better for you. Observe slowly as you move upwards that actually your head rocks and your chin goes away from the sternum at least a little bit. With some the chin moves sufficiently away that you can see it from far away, and with some you have to look very closely to see whether they really move the chin or not.

Now again do a few discrete movements upwards, but with an accent. Push and stop; let go and push again upward. You will see that the chin must go away or the head slides on the floor. Now why do you let the head slide on the floor? Again, you'll find someone in the group will not know that he or she lets the head slide on the floor and therefore what I said about the chin just doesn't ring a bell. I ask again, why do you let the back of the head slide on the floor? Push upwards—it slides on the floor. Now the person to whom I speak, who has the head sliding on the floor, is the only one who doesn't know what I'm talking about. So please hold your chin fixed to your body so it doesn't move. Now rock and you will see that the back of the head will slide on the floor. If you put a piece of chalk there, it would mark a little line on the floor. Now move your pelvis and your whole head in such a way that this little line is not drawn; that means your head will rock around the point where it touches the floor just like the pelvis.

Would you stop that, all of you—except you. That's it, you stay there. Now, would you please rock your pelvis now, as we did, pulling the legs. Now look, can you see? The only head that doesn't rock. I explained the movement of the head already half a dozen times; and explained to you that it will describe a little line—if it slides on the floor. How could you not understand all the things we said up till now? Now, would you please sit up. I can make you say the correct thing but you don't understand it. That's how we learn at school; that's scholastic learning. We hear it, we can repeat it, we can write it down and we don't know what we're doing. Now fortunately some people in school get some sort of personal experience and say, 'Ah! I got the trick. I know it.' And some teachers have the knack of appealing to some of the pupils—they don't know how. And therefore the whole world is not idiotic. But on the average, yes.

[Moshé asks one person to continue.]

Now would you please lie down and continue to rock your pelvis. By the way, your head moved very faintly, about a quarter of the range of movement of the others. Now the rest of you watch what she does, and you will learn something important. Notice what her head does, and her chin. When she draws her pelvis down, and the angle behind her knee joint gets smaller, her chin goes to her chest. And when the angle gets bigger so that the coccyx is lifted and the lumbar spine touches the floor, her chin goes away from her sternum. Now if you think she does a special trick, someone try it.

[Three groups members lie on the floor and try the movement. But they slide their heads on the floor.] Oh-hhh, can you see? If you don't know what you're doing then, you're not doing what you want, but something else. Now, look, she is sliding now—she can't do it. (laughter) [Moshé speaks to the other two people demonstrating.] Now, would you do it? No, you're moving your chin away intentionally. That's rubbish. Do what you did before; go down and go up. Go fast. And then go so fast that you have no time to have stage fright (laughter). And now, that's it. Look what a change. Now, would you all imitate her [the person Moshé first asked to go to the floor] and make the movement so that you do not move your head. All the three are now doing what you intend. I call that learning when you can do the same thing in two different ways; then you have a choice.

Now *they* have the choice; they have bought a car that can go forward and in reverse too; which is a more useful car than one that can go forward only.

Now lie down and *you* make the choices; let it go so your

chin moves—and arrange your body so that your chin stays as it is, and the back of your head slides on the floor. When you know what you're doing, you have free choice, and a human way of acting. Learning involves gaining a difference, and it must be a *significant* difference.

Now, try again and make two movements as you did. Now how will you do it the other way? You see, you actually lift your head a little bit and bring it a little bit nearer to yourself. Make it easy and keep on doing it. If you watch the person we saw before, whose chin did not move, she holds her head now. This is what stops her movement. In her life she was instructed by her school to *sit straight*. She got it so straight that she forgot how she does it and it's now compulsive and somewhere in her unconscious. She therefore has no access to the muscles of her neck.

Again let us all do what she did and what you did. And you will discover what I mean by free choice and learning *another* way. It's so simple that nobody stumbles over it. Now make a clear difference between the two possibilities. You slide your head and then let it rock. But it *is* better; there's *some* movement. Now you will see: don't move your pelvis, but move your head without sliding. You will put the back of your head in such a place that you can rock it. Can you do it without moving the pelvis? If you don't move your pelvis your head slides on the floor. So there is a connection between your head sliding on the floor, and your pelvis not moving. In fact, this trouble, of which you are not aware, permeates your entire activity. If you examine her many movements, you'll find fifty different acts that she does improperly; and improperly means much less well than she can do now. In fifteen minutes she can improve everything if she becomes aware of what she's doing and what she's not doing. And that's what we're doing now— we're saving her soul; we're missionaries.

All right now, would you please move your head so that it doesn't slide, and find that it is essentially impossible to rock without letting the pelvis rock also. Otherwise you have to make your body such a stiff structure that the power produced is absorbed in those stiff joints held by your muscles. The muscles don't yield and therefore you don't feel them. Move your head and you will see that the pelvis does exactly the same. How could it do otherwise? If your head and pelvis are stuck together with a stick, could you move one without moving the other?

Now we have done everything to make our spine lie almost like a stick; in that direction it has no flexibility at all. The top of the pelvis lies on the floor. Therefore if you move the pelvis the head must move. Now try; if you don't slide your head, then you cannot rock your head without rocking your pelvis.

Would you please stretch your right leg and continue the same movement; notice the difference. Now your pelvis can't rock the way it did before. You should now be clear that the top moves up and down. Make the movement only with the left leg on the floor; let your right leg do what it wants.

If we want to make sure that every person has learned the same amount in that lesson, then that lesson must be three to four times as long. The rate of learning is absolutely personal. In the whole group I find two or three who learn the greatest amount and a few who learn the least amount and many in between. In the in-between group are many people who have been taught since childhood that to use themselves *must* be difficult and it must be uncomfortable. They will find about 100 different restrictions that they impose on themselves without knowing. They can't do the movement easily and therefore learn less than the others. If we wanted the slow ones to learn with us, then we must have patience while those who are slow and impose restrictions on themselves are corrected. We have not spoken about these restrictions, which the situation doesn't demand. Restriction is a compulsive habit of ignoring one's own comfort. It's a lifelong problem. One learns things not because they're pleasant, comfortable, make you feel well, but because you *have* to. When you have to, you do it; it doesn't matter how.

All right then, with your left leg still standing put your right leg over the left. This is my way of getting the people who don't feel to understand. Now, take your left leg another 10 inches to the left. Only those who need to do it, do it. That is because some of you put the left foot in front of the left buttock. Try it over to your right, and you will see, the rocking will not be so different from before—it will be up and down. When it's more up and down, you feel it. Therefore, move your left foot a bit to the left, put the right leg crossed over the left and continue the rocking movement of the pelvis. That's right. Now note, what part of your pelvis remains on the floor when you push? Or you could find which side of the pelvis is clear on the floor, and which side of the pelvis does not lie so intimately connected with the floor. And now, which shoulder moves when you push with your left leg? Which shoulder blade moves more? Which clavicle moves more? If you want to know, lift your left shoulder off the floor with the left side of the chest and keep on doing the movement. Put your left hand over your body so the left shoulder blade is lifted from the floor. Now, as you are, turn your chest so that your right shoulder blade doesn't touch the floor, and continue to rock. Now, which shoulder is moved? Which shoulder hinders you? Which shoulder can you lift without trouble, and without interfering with the movement? Can you feel that it's your right shoulder that moves? And therefore, can you feel how the effort of the hip joint is transmitted through the spine to the right shoulder blade?

If you want to really feel the difference, turn your face with your chin as close to your left clavicle as possible. Continue rocking, and you see it gets even better. Now, turn your head with your chin to the right clavicle. As you continue, you will feel the movement in your head, and feel that your right shoulder is moving more than the left. But your head is actually doing as much as your shoulder. It is a pronounced movement of about 5 cm on the floor.

Stop. Stretch both legs and both arms on the floor. Feel through which part of yourself the power was transmitted from the hip joint to the right shoulder blade. Put your left foot standing; put the right leg crossed over the left and do it again. Notice now that your spine twists from the left hip joint to the right shoulder blade and the right side of the chest (the ribs) tries to lie on the floor on points that are not normally in contact. Someone who had a hunchback would feel that very clearly. The left side is the other way around; the floating ribs near the spine, are lifted from the floor. Your chest is trying to soften from right and left.

Now, would you slowly turn on your right side, stretching your right arm overhead. But keep your legs crossed as they are. And as you stand on your legs as before, rock your pelvis. But don't turn to the right before it's possible. Do small movements until you feel that you can actually straighten your right arm. For many it's not straight in the elbow, it's not straight in the shoulder. Slowly rock the body because your chest will deform and allow your shoulder blade to move and you'll find that your right hand actually slides on the floor with every movement of the pelvis. And if you help yourself by rotating and rolling your chest so that the diagonal movement goes clearly through your entire spine, your right arm will lie better and better, and straighten more and more.

Now keep on rolling to the right in as much as you continue to improve and the right side of your chest allows you. And now notice: you have to suddenly put your right hip joint also on the floor with the same quality as the left. And your legs stand as before. Your knees move neither right nor left, but are not stationary because your pelvis is moving. It doesn't matter if you don't roll properly. It's enough that you learn that it can be done and that the movement connects your pelvis, head, and chest. You will improve sufficiently.

Now, lift your left hand, and keep your right hand where it is. Lift your left hand to the ceiling. Continue rocking, and let your left hand gradually sink to the right and sink another degree. Don't exceed more than 1 degree for each movement, so that it takes ninety movements.

Now continue lifting your left shoulder blade and the left side of your chest and you will realize how much work this movement does on the right side of your chest, including your ribs and all twelve vertebrae and the lumbar region, and your neck. In fact your spine tries to learn how to move vertebra after vertebra so that you can roll on the right side. Your right arm will become longer and straighter, and the chest softer and stronger. And you will see that actually the amount of stretch that is now happening in the right arm and the shoulder blades is so great that when you stop that you'll have to take your right arm down carefully or else it will be painful because the muscles of your shoulder have been enlarging the margin of movement near to what they were built to be able to do.

Now stop; bring your arm back to rest. Stretch and you will see that if you bring your right arm back up, you will take it on the side, sliding on the floor. Otherwise it is painful. You can feel there was a change in your shoulder joint that was very significant. A quick movement would be very painful. Stretch your arm and lift it back but don't slide your elbow on the floor. Can you feel the change that occurred in the shoulder blade and the clavicle? Of course if you do a few movements it's lost again.

Lie on your right side. Would you please stretch your right arm, put your left foot standing, stretch your right leg. Put your left hand on the right side of your chest on the floor as if for pushing up. That's right. Note how the right arm lies and the right elbow and the back of the hand. And now using your left leg, with your knee pointing to the ceiling or as nearly as you can get to this position without effort, push your pelvis as we did, but you must lie nearly on the right side. Your left hand is standing on the floor for pushing up. You can't do the movement unless you lie on your right side. Continue to rock your pelvis with your left leg and watch what your pelvis does. Can you feel the movement in your right hand? You don't have to contract the right leg at all, or push with the right leg. Rock like butter, like jelly, like creme caramel. Now observe how the small ribs of your right side touch the floor and move away. Obviously something happens in your spine to make that possible. The lower ribs move to a greater degree than the

others, and your floating ribs should move more. Can you feel
how the middle of the body touches and goes away? Notice
what your hand feels like now, how it lies on the floor. And
remember how it was before. Your head and face are turned
toward the right. Each movement makes you feel that your
shoulder blades must make a fine adjustment in the relationship to allow your arm to go up. We got some inkling of that
before, but at that time we didn't think much of the change.
Remember we did that when we made a full circle with the
arm. But at that time we lifted the pelvis and chest to slide our
hand underneath.

Now slowly lie on your back. Observe how your right arm
lies now; you can see there's a tremendous change in the
shoulder blade, the clavicle and all the intercostal muscles
behind and in front of the right side of your chest. And if you
bend both legs and cross your right leg over your left, keep
your right arm where it was, and now rock your pelvis, you
will see how your right shoulder and right arm move more
directly. But also observe what your chest does *now*. There's
a new movement in your shoulder and arm resulting from the
fact that your chest is deforming itself to allow that movement. Stop and lie like that; stretch the left arm and lower the
right and notice the difference. Where is it? The difference is
in the part of yourself that connects the pelvis to the shoulder
blades; it is throughout the spine and the chest. Now stretch
out, put your arms alongside the body. Observe the difference.

Alright now, would you please do the following: stretch your
left arm over your head and put the right foot standing, and
think, without moving, of how the pressure on your foot tries
to move the floor under you, and lifts the right hip joint. What
sort of change should you feel in your chest? How much should
you roll to the left before your left arm will straighten? Now
roll to the left side completely, and with your right hand on
the floor make that see-saw movement of the stomach, abdomen, and chest. Now roll to the right in the same symmetrical
position, change the leg which is standing, and do the same
rocking. Observe how different it is on this side. And now

notice this: the deformation of the chest makes it so that the stomach muscles and the chest muscles on this side don't move. Slowly draw your abdomen in and expand your chest—and reverse. Observe how much you can move with your stomach and chest.

Now turn onto the other side—symmetrically—and observe that on this side the stomach muscles and the chest are different. The impression you may have is that the stomach muscles are either working harder or not obeying you on one of the sides. If I tell you which, you will merely be exercising. *You* find how the chest obeys you now, how the stomach obeys you now, when you alternate one side or the other. With each change from side to side they become more equal. Go to the other side and feel. But find finer differences of sensation, because there is very little doubt that the stomach muscles on one side can work easier and with less effort. Here the lower ribs and pelvis have organized themselves so they lie on the floor.

Now lie on the other side and look again for the same details. In this you have a chance for real change from what it was before you did the lesson.

Now lie on your stomach. Put both hands on either side of your body as if you were going to do a push-up, and flex your feet so the toes stand on the floor. Put your head more or less in the middle. Lift your head a little bit, so that your nose and chin do not rub the floor. Your elbows are in the air. Now push with your feet and make a similar rocking movement; as you push with your feet your pelvis rocks, pushes the spine, and your shoulders and head move forward. Now, put your forehead on the floor; the movement now rocks your head. But don't *press* the floor with your forehead. Rock a few times, each time lighter. You needn't repeat the movement many times because you know it already. Make one discrete movement; watch what happens with your stomach and chest, when you push and and when you let go. Can you feel that the whole spine is pushed forward and rocks your head? Why didn't it happen with some people when they lay on their backs? Do that many times. Now lift your forehead off the floor one quarter inch, without changing position; just lift it so that it doesn't touch. Continue! Can you see now there is no rocking of your head? In other words, when your head doesn't rock the muscles of your neck are stiff and don't know how to move at all and never let go.

Now put your forehead on the floor and notice that it *does* rock. And in fact the amount of rocking is not equal with everybody; there are different rates. So keep on moving like that, pushing with your feet, but put your shoulders closer to the floor, when you push forward, and then lift them. Your hands are in the position for pushing up. When you push forward, move your head and shoulders downwards, and also your spine between the shoulders. We learned before to sink it downwards; now push it down, slowly, and when you let the body go back, lift. Now, at least five times put both tips of the shoulders down while you push forward. You will find that unless you move your elbows forward you don't make this movement. Each time you push with your feet let the elbows go forward, and the whole shoulder girdle, sternum and clavicles included, tend to go to the floor. Lift your forehead and continue the movement. Then put your chin on the floor while pushing, and then the tips of the shoulders will go to the floor. Do it several times.

As you continue pushing with your feet, now lift the tips of your shoulders backwards as much as you can. Your elbows should go nearer to the floor. Also lift your sternum, but your head and chin stay on the floor. The sternum and the whole cervical spine must move, and you will find that your head now rocks on the chin a tremendous amount. Continue to push forward and push the shoulders, but now we lift the shoulders. Lowering and lifting are different. How does your head move? Can you see that it rocks in such a way that your forehead moves away from the floor? Now stand like that with your chin on the floor and don't move your shoulders but push with your feet, and rock yourself to see whether your head rocks and how much.

Now stop and begin the movement alternating stomach and chest. Observe whether the right side of your stomach presses on the floor as much as the left, and also whether the right side of your breast presses on the floor the same way as the left. Continue and make sure that only the right side of the abdomen touches. Cross your right leg over the left; the knee too, if possible. Now push and make sure that you push the floor with the left side of your abdomen. That's the only easy way to do it. As you do that, see which side of your chest presses harder. Which breast rubs the floor? And also which hand presses on the floor harder? Without thinking. Now, put your forehead on the floor and continue to rock and see whether the rocking of your head has increased or decreased. Now you feel the left side of the abdomen pressing on the floor. Put your legs normally and spread them. Use both feet. And now intentionally press the left side on the floor. Push with both feet and make the left side clear. Can you feel that the right side is pressing less? Turn to make the right side move as clearly as the left. It's not so easy because the movements we did previously were not symmetrical. You have to change your chest to allow yourself to feel the stomach muscles on that side acting as powerfully as on the other.

Stop; lie on your back. Bend your legs. Note how it feels in your back, your chest, your shoulder blades. Slowly rock your pelvis through your legs, and see how different it is. Now it's normal. *All* heads rock properly. Would you please just look at the person who had no choice before? Look at her now. Can you see that she's not sillier than you or I? It was only a question that this movement was completely unfamiliar to her. Therefore you could talk from today until tomorrow, explain all the anatomy and use all your gestalt therapy and any other therapy, and she would just show incredible resistance to adjusting herself to reality. Improper functioning and improper thinking go *by* the phenomenon, they don't correct it. They correct only a minor angle, a minor facet. Here she has learned the two functions. She can do the movement two ways and has a choice. Her freedom has increased. She has shifted her possibility from a compulsion to a deliberate decision. What can be better treatment than that?

Would you please get up a little bit and walk around and have a break. Observe, of course, what feels new. I recommend this especially to the person who has regained the choice. Can you see it's not a question of exercising?

Thank you. (applause)

LESSON TWELVE:
LEARNING TO SIT FROM LYING

We're going to do a fast movement using what you have learned so we can distinguish between speed and hurry. A person in a hurry is a person that realizes that he or she is too slow. If he weren't too slow there would be no need to hurry. For a person who's in a hurry, you can be sure that inwardly that person feels, "I am slow, I'm no bloody good." And you will find that there is a disturbance that permeates the whole being. Steckel, a major general in the Austrian Army, was one of those psychiatrists whom Freud thought as good as Adler. He was one of Freud's first four students. Steckel was more important and better known than Freud. His two most important books (there are many) are *Impotence in Men* and *Frigidity in Women.* In both books, he says, impotence in men and frigidity in women happens in people who have no connection with time. They are in a hurry. Thus, if you correct the time relationship for a person, the sexual trouble disappears. You don't have to do anything else. Some people have discovered it themselves, through Awareness Through Movement. They experienced a change of personality and the ability to rid themselves of the sexual difficulty. One can improve for the rest of one's life. The idea is to be able to distinguish between hurry and time. Take your time. If you can't take your time you're in a hurry and you know that you're no good. So now we're going to lose our notion of time and go fast—but distinguish between fast and hurry.

Would you please lie on your stomach. Bend both knees, and join your knees and feet. Imagine you have two large rubber bands and put one of them at the knees and one at the ankles to hold your legs together. With your knees and ankles so tied together in your imagination, move them as they are a little bit to the right and a little bit to the left. Now increase that movement and see whether your head and shoulders and arms are interfering with the movement. Organize your hands and arms and head and observe; if you have your head to the left, is the movement easier to the left or to the right? Therefore turn your head so that if your legs go to the right your head lies to the left with your right cheek on the floor. Now, wait a minute. Begin to tilt but move your head, shoulder, and arms in such a way that you can see your heels from the corner of your eye.

You don't look under your stomach; look there and you can find only your sex. Look to your heels. Where are they? They're in the air. So your eyes must go into the air, but not from underneath your arm. Why not put both hands on the floor as you would for pushing up? But why do it in such an awkward way? Well, you will learn in a minute that if it's awkward like that it will be slow, ugly to see, and difficult for you. Slowly, lift your head and turn your shoulders and use your arms to see the heels. [Moshé shouts.] *Don't let the heels move unless you can see them.* Then watch them and follow them until they lie on the floor. *See them on the floor!* Now that is *shouting* for you to go fast and light; it's ordering about. And what are you learning? Who told you that you can learn comfortably like that? In life it is, "Would you *move?* Or not?" Or, "You're out!" You will see the kind of learning we'll get with that.

Alright now, lie on your stomach, and put your hands as if for pushing up. Look at your heels as you lift your head and tilt your legs until you can see your heels lying on the floor. Notice how you use your arms. Now lie back again. Repeat this movement three or four times and think: how you would do it on the other side? Continue on this side until your thinking about the other side is clear in the light of your experience on this side. And now go ahead and move to both sides. Increase the speed, the simplicity of the movement. Now you will sit up in order to see your heels. If you don't sit up, there is no use screwing up your face; you won't see your heels. It's simple. It must be general. The whole body must cooperate uniformly. Place your hands so that you *can* sit up. What about your right hand? What about your legs? Can you sit up while you tilt your legs? Why straighten them? As you continue, discover that one arm is not needed for you to sit up. Continue and make it useless each time. But it won't be useless unless you sit properly. So how will we do that? Now see if you can divorce the knees. You keep your knees close because the buttocks are so close to each other and there's only one little passage between them. The two buttocks quarrel over the hole of the anus— they never agree and are always two opposites. Silly buttocks, no?

Continue, but go slow. This time we're going to learn how to let go of the other arm. Stop holding your knees together; take off one of the rubber bands and then the other one too. And now do the same movement as before but separate your knees while sitting up, so that you can see both heels; then you take one leg behind the other one.

Now lie and when you sit up, do the same movement again. If you continue that movement and watch your heels, you don't need the other arm. It gets useless. Use both arms and sit up again and you will discover you can sit without either arm. You can let them go together with the legs. And spread your knees more to help. Now you sit properly without your hands.

Move them back again and imagine that you're going to do the same thing on the other side. Now you must pay attention to the person on each side of you. If you don't you will bang into the other person when you try the movement. Now don't say a *word* and don't think a thing. I could say, "All of you: go to your left!" Then you will be organized. But what will you learn? Therefore if you speak in order to organize with your neighbor, and say 'Let's see now, we go together.' That's like music. Music is very funny thing. Many think it heightens the soul, improves the mind, and makes you feel so human. But *music* was used to burn Jews! And the people who did it were of the most musical country in the world. They let *some* Jews survive to play while the others were burned. So your refined music is *bunkum.* Music doesn't refine *anybody.* But of course a non-violent person can also make good music. But it's not the music that makes the man. Music can be wonderful. And it can be the dirtiest thing in the world.

Now if you want to organize yourselves to move together, do it humanly. Don't use music. Don't use orders. Don't do anything, just feel, and sense the person next to you. Please lie on your stomach and *don't talk!* Begin to move and *feel* where the people are. Both your hands go free if you *spread* your knees sufficiently and take one knee back enough and the other one forward enough. Hey you backwards beauty—your legs are not right—you must learn to open your legs properly. It's a very important function for a woman. That's better. Move *both* hands on this side and *both* hands on the other. Swing—*every particle* in you should swing.

[Moshé corrects someone who organizes well on one side and not the other.]

What you do is "hurrying." The pelvis must move as we learned before, so that it is left to roll in a continuous, smooth curve. Then your hands and legs know where to go. Pay attention to your pelvis and head and look at your heels. Watch his movement—he's very clever; *now* he move his pelvis all right. Before he jerked it. That's still not good enough. Lying on the floor you should not hit the bones of the pelvis. You hit your left iliac. Not enough to hurt, but if you do a million movements like that, it will be *blue.* Now look, when you swing, the forward part of your pelvis does this—so-oooo; it doesn't do this—'pang.' Don't do 'pang.' If it does 'pang' it means you have stretched your leg. Try slowly. If you move your leg back enough then you roll on the stomach and not on the iliacs. Rolling on your iliacs interferes with your going fast whether you know it or not. Our nervous system has a very long experience in this world. It knows when you have to sneeze, and when you have to take the legs, and where to roll. It's only our intelligence that makes us do the idiotic thing. Now that's better.

Would you stop a minute? After we will see what sort of speed you can get up to. You'll try any other way of sitting and lying and see if you can achieve that speed. I say with that speed you do it faster than a cat. Would you please lie on your stomach and start when I give a signal. But if you don't look at each other while starting and don't *feel* each other, you will bang into each other. And now, breathing freely, remember what Stekel told you—that hurry and speed are two different things. One is a bloody nuisance and one is the greatest pleasure in life. Start. And the hands, *and* the legs, *and* the chest, *and* the mustache, and everything you have should swing the same way. Now that's beautiful. Can you see—ah!—can you see how you now sit to the left? You know why? Because you organize yourself with two people. By yourself, it would take you a *month* to organize the left side as the right. That is because you have a trouble. But consider this: your nervous system has learned to act properly from the start. A child experiences his own urge to do something, and with his senses he moves in the world finding objects from the outside which allow learning and meaning to take place. And this learning must be social, otherwise one becomes an autistic or schizophrenic and is put away. If the social function is not smooth, then the movement of the person cannot adapt to the purpose of real life in our society. If you have to deal with real biological, and physiological trouble, unless you understand *that,* you cannot improve, you cannot heal the person. You can *kill* germs with drugs but the person won't be able to function properly.

Now *you* watch and observe how much your left side has improved through moving in coordination with your two neighbors. Lie on your stomach and all three of you do it again. Now it's a *challenge* and therefore you should do it *badly.* (laughter) No one watches. Now watch—here is a person who has a difficulty on one side of her body. She was annoyed with it the Thursday she came. Look how she does it to the left—

look how she does it to the right, and tell me: which is her bad side? Which is the good one? You can see she moves as well as anyone else and equally on both sides. Therefore she owes me a kiss. (laughter and applause) No, I don't ask for it *now*—you give it when *I* want it.

Would you please now, lie down and find out that the social function is not just a nuisance; it improves our physiology. If you don't know that, you are not a good social person even if you go to the synagogue or church seven times a week. As a social being, all our brain is used, including inherited qualities as well as animal qualities. We produce a freedom in the brain, which frees our hands and gives us the possibility of reforming the left hemisphere, where we have the functions of writing, speaking and reading. Therefore our biological, our physiological and social living is interconnected; for the human species it is life.

Often people are asked, what would you do if you had to live the rest of your life all alone on an island? What would you take, what books, what records? Now I would advise you like this,: throw the books and records into the sea. You need something *more of yourself to be alive.*

We tend not to realize that a social life is not only a social life, but a biological, physiological necessity. We could not exist a day without it. Just to escape from humanity one needs something of humanity. Even to kill yourself you would need a pistol or some pills made by others. In fact we can not live or die but as social beings. People are just becoming aware of it. For example medical people are now realizing that to heal a person with multiple sclerosis, the social functions of that person need to be organized properly.

We are not alone. We act always with the knowledge that there is an observer. We are born of a mother and come into the world with an observer, with another being. You should consider the importance of that for the rest of your life. And so the relations between us and other people and the objects we make, use and play with, and with the entire social world, improves our physiology.

In depression too people relate to things of the social world or to others. Some may buy a hat that they never wear. But picking the hat that suits one takes away the depression. Others have an intimate relation with someone. It doesn't matter how close the intimacy is and whether it is real or not—but it is better than being alone. That's why some miserable people live together—because it's better than being alone.

Now if it's better than being alone then roll here on the floor —not as if you were alone. Lie on your stomach, and without looking, feel in your entire being how far the next person is from you—whether that person is a man or a woman. You *can* feel it and if you pay attention you will find that you *know* it. Now, begin the movement. Obviously the beginning must be a little bit slow if the others should pick rhythm. But it doesn't matter; if you go fast, the others can wait until they find it possible. Watch now—Nancy does it now better than many of you. Those who fail do so because they don't allow themselves to go slower. They should stop. All the slow movers, go slow —try to move as slowly as your own rhythm. Eliminate all the things that interfere with your going fast. Slowly, one after the other, eliminate the minor errors in using your hands, in bending your legs, and so on. Go as slow as you need to *feel* the things which you are not doing really well for yourself. The failure is social in origin. Those who feel so nice socially think that to go slow means to be lowered socially. It feels like an inner insult to them and they refuse to do it. Therefore they try to go faster than they can. Go slow so you can become as fast as anyone. Go so slow that you can eliminate everything that is unnecessary. Move your knees apart more. Your speed will increase by itself. And it will get better if you do it together with the persons around you. Then your speed will go to the limit of human ability. And why do you stop? Why not make it into a continuous movement? Can you see? There are so many stumbling blocks—so many inhibitions. That means you make restrictions for yourself that are not necessary if you desire to go fast. That's why to become a gold medalist it's not important to spend hours on running, but on examining in oneself useless action.

All right now, *everybody* go so slow that the slowest person has time to do the movement. Move in honey, or in mud. And you will see when you move slowly that the really important thing is to have the same quality of mobilization throughout the body. And that's the quality for going fast.

Swing your hands too. Swing and bring both arms into movement. Your head *and* shoulders, and *everything* should swing as far and as well as you need.

Now, I think we have enough of that. So you see that we can move fast too. And you see that moving fast has a greater significance. Being faster than somebody else is a minor achievement. But to know fast or slow in oneself is extraordinary—not only as a physiological function—but in human relations, in sexual relations, in other relations. Whether you're in a hurry, or give yourself the leisure to act at your own pace—is of immense significance. Anyway you're clever enough now yourself. Thank you. (applause)

BOOK LIST
Meta Publications Inc
P.O. Box 565
Cupertino, Ca. 95015

The Master Moves. $20.00
Moshe Feldenkrais

Magic in Action $14.95
Richard Bandler

Roots of Neuro-Linguistic Programming $22.00
Robert Dilts (hardcover)

Applications of Neuro-Linguistic Programming $22.00
Robert Dilts (hardcover)

Meta-Cation: Prescriptions for Some Ailing Educational Processes $12.00
Sid Jacobson (hardcover)

Phoenix—Therapeutic Patterns of Milton H. Erickson. $14.00
D. Gordon & M. Myers-Anderson (hardcover)

Neuro-Linguistic Programming. $24.00
Dilts, Grinder, Bandler et al
Limited Edition (hardcover)

The Elusive Obvious $20.00
Moshe Feldenkrais (deluxe edition)

Patterns of Hypnotic Techniaues of Milton H. Erickson, M.D. . . . $8.95
Bandler and Grinder
Volume I (paper only)

Patterns of Hypnotic Techniques of Milton H. Erickson, M.D. . . . $17.95
Bandler, DeLozier, Grinder
Volume II (hardcover)

Provocative Therapy $10.95
Farrelly & Brandsma (hardcover)

Gestalt Therapy and Beyond $9.95
Marcus (hardcover)

Changing With Families $9.95
Bandler, Grinder and Satir (hardcover)

The Structure of Magic, Volume 1. . . . . $8.95
Bandler and Grinder (paper)

The Structure of Magic, Volume II $8.95
Bandler and Grinder (paper)

Practical Magic $12.00
Stephen R. Lankton (hardcover)

Therapeutic Metaphors. $10.95
David Gordon (hardcover)